food & drink

SERVICE IN THE RESTAURANT

NVQ

WORKBOOK LEVEL 2

SVQ

SARAH MACLEOD & FIONA DOUGLAS

Food Studies Department

Edinburgh's Telford College

Hodder & Stoughton

A MEMBER OF THE HODDER HEADLINE GROUP

A catalogue record for this title is available from the British Library

ISBN 0 340 61151 0

First published 1994
Impression number 10   9   8   7   6   5   4   3   2   1
Year   1999   1998   1997   1996   1995   1994

Typeset by Wearset, Boldon, Tyne and Wear.
Printed in Great Britain for Hodder & Stoughton Educational, a division of
Hodder Headline Plc, 338 Euston Road, London NW1 3BH by
Bath Press, Avon

CONTENTS

Unit G1

MAINTAIN A SAFE AND SECURE WORKING
ENVIRONMENT

Fire prevention

Fire safety is a serious business. Fires in hotel and catering establishments are common and all too often can result in injury to the employee and in serious cases either injury or loss of life to employees and customers.

A basic knowledge regarding fire should assist in preventing fires and handling them if they do occur. Three components are necessary for a fire to start; if one of the three is not present or is removed then the fire does not happen or is extinguished.

The three points are:
- fuel – something to burn;
- air – oxygen to sustain combustion (to keep the fire going);
- heat – gas, electricity etc.

METHODS OF EXTINGUISHING A FIRE

To extinguish a fire the three principal methods are:
- starving – removing the fuel;
- smothering – removing the air (oxygen);
- cooling – removing the heat.

Therefore one of the sides of the triangle is removed:

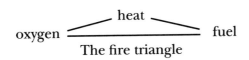

The fire triangle

❖ **Remember**
1 You should familiarise yourself with the extinguishers and fire-fighting equipment at your place of work, before an emergency arises.
2 Fire extinguishers must not be removed until you need to use them.
3 After an extinguisher has been used, it should be replaced by a new extinguisher as soon as possible and the used extinguisher should be recharged by the manufacturer.
4 In heat and smoke the best conditions are to be found near the floor.
5 Breathe through the nose to filter out particles of carbon.
6 Keep your actions as effortless as possible in order to reduce the amount of air and

hence the amount of smoke drawn into the lungs.

7 Go backwards down the ladders and stairs so that the face is protected from the rising heat.

8 Cloths over the nose and mouth may remove some of the larger particles of carbon but they give **no** protection whatsoever against oxygen deficiency and they do tend to give a false sense of security.

❖ **Safety does not happen, it is the reward of care, thought and good organisation.**

WHAT TO DO IN CASE OF FIRE

When you hear the fire alarm, go immediately to the specified assembly point and be prepared to help if required. If you discover a fire and cannot extinguish it, immediately:

1 Close the door to keep the fire and smoke in the room.
2 Sound the fire alarm.
3 Make sure that the Fire Brigade is called without delay and advise the management.
4 Proceed to the appropriate fire or assembly point.
5 Start a 'roll call'.

It is important that in all catering establishments, passageways are kept clear and the doors open outwards. Fire escape doors and windows should be clearly marked and fire-fighting equipment must be readily available and in working order. Periodic fire drills should occur. Fire alarm bells must be tested at least four times a year and staff should be instructed in the use of fire-fighting equipment. This section has only been a guideline for fire prevention procedures. For more specific advice, contact your local Fire Prevention Officer.

ELEMENT G1.1 *Carry out procedures in the event of a fire*

In the event of a fire:

1 How do you raise the alarm?

....

....

....

2   List the fire-fighting equipment in your place of work.

a) Fire extinguishers

Colour	*Number*	*Suitable for type of fire*
Red	....	
Black	....	
Green	....	

b) Fire blankets (number) ....

3   Are there any signs telling you what to do in case of fire?   Yes ☐   No ☐
If there are, what do they say?

....

....

....

....

....

....

4   Briefly, write down what you have to do in the case of fire.

a) ....

b) ....

c) ....

d) ....

5   Where do you go to in case of fire?

....

....

6   Who do you report to when you get there?

....

....

❖ **If there is either a fire drill, false alarm or actual fire you must make a note of the date and what you did.**

ELEMENT G1.2   *Carry out procedures on the discovery of a suspicious item or package*

1   What should you do if you find a suspicious package?

....

....

....

2   Ask your supervisor if the company has a procedure for dealing with suspicious packages. If there is you should make note of what it is.

....

....

3   If there is not a policy statement, who should you inform on finding a suspicious package?

....

....

....

❖ **If you find a suspicious package at work, make a note of the date and what you did.**

First aid

The Health and Safety (First Aid) Regulations 1981, cover an employer's responsibilities to his or her employees. Under the Act, an employer must:
*   make First Aid provision for employees who may be injured at work;
*   appoint First Aiders, or provide people capable of dealing with an incident if First Aiders are not available.

A First Aider is a person who has obtained a First Aid certificate within the past three years, from an approved organisation, e.g. St Andrew's Ambulance Association, British Red Cross Society.

CONTENTS OF A FIRST AID BOX

A First Aid Box should be marked with a white cross on a green background. The **minimum** legally required contents are listed in the table below.

Item	Number of employees				
	1–5	6–10	11–50	51–100	101–150
Guidance card	1	1	1	1	1
Individually wrapped sterile adhesive dressing	10	20	40	40	40
Sterile eye-pad with attachment	1	2	4	6	8
Triangular bandage	1	2	4	6	8
Sterile covering for serious wounds (where applicable)	1	2	4	6	8
Safety pins	6	6	12	12	12
Medium sized sterile (unmedicated) dressing	3	6	8	10	12
Large sterile (unmedicated) dressing	1	2	4	6	10
Extra large sterile (unmedicated) dressing	1	2	4	6	10

Food Hygiene (General) Regulations 1970, require that caterers must also supply waterproof dressing (blue for food handlers).

For more advice contact your Health and Safety Executive or Local Authority. They will be able to give you advice relating to your own place of work and the requirements of the law.

ACCIDENT REPORTING

All businesses should keep records of accidents, however apparently slight, and the following report could be used:

Accident report	
Name of injured person	
Time and date of accident	
Time and date of report	
Nature of injury	
Was a hospital visit required?	
Was medical help needed?	
Report of injury by medical personnel	
Place of accident	
Evidence of injured person (include account of equipment or other people involved)	
Accounts of witnesses: 1 2	
Any other comments or recommendations by supervisor	
Date: Supervisor's Signature:	

ACCIDENT PREVENTION

Each year, more than 4000 injuries occur in the catering and allied industries. Most of these accidents are falls and burns, and many of them could be avoided.

- Plan the working environment so that potentially dangerous activities are kept within a restricted area: place cookers near sinks and tables so that pans containing hot liquids do not have to be carried across traffic areas.
- Use the equipment provided in the correct way, e.g. do not remove guards from machines.
- Consider the effect that your actions may have on the safety of others, e.g. wipe up spills immediately so that no-one is likely to slip.

GUIDELINES FOR LIFTING MATERIALS AND GOODS

- Use thigh, not back muscles to effect the lift.
- Squat down, weight on ball of foot, otherwise flat on ground for stability, knees apart.
- Obtain firm hold on load by using full palm grip. Keep elbows and load close to body.
- Ensure back is straight (not necessarily vertical). Keep chin in to align vertebrae, and then use thigh muscles to do the lifting.
- Do not twist body whilst lifting. Pivot on ball of foot after lifting. Avoid over-reaching.
- In effecting a two-man lift, the above principles should be followed but the lift should be commenced on a given signal.
- If a load is too heavy for you, summon assistance. Do not rush into lifting a potentially heavy object. Try the weight gently first. Recognise your lifting capability and do not exceed it.
- Plan each lift for safety.
- Avoid wearing rings whilst handling materials. Do wear protective gloves if the item you are lifting has sharp projections on it.

❖ **Remember**

The above is only a list of guidelines. If you are in any doubt about the correct procedures contact your local Health and Safety Executive or Local Authority.

ELEMENT G1.3 *Carry out procedures in the event of an accident*

1 Ask your supervisor who you should tell if you or somebody else you are working with has an accident.

....

....

2 Where is the first aid box?

....

....

3 How do you deal with a person who has cut themselves?

....

....

4 How do you deal with a burn or scald?

....

....

5 How do you deal with a person in shock?

....

....

6 What should you do if a person is electrocuted?

....

....

7   What is the purpose of the accident book?

....

....

❖ **Remember**

Any accidents you have or witness should be recorded.

Health and safety legislation

Health and Safety covers not only the personnel and environmental hygiene issues but the health and safety of employers, employees and customers. This comes under the Health and Safety at Work Act 1974 (HASAWA). It is the statutory duty of everyone at work to care for the health and safety of everyone in the workplace – colleagues or customers. Everyone at work, or affected by the work, e.g. customers, is protected under the Act. This means that **everyone** in the workplace is affected by the legislation:

- Employers
- Self-employed
- Employees
- Contractors
- Trainees, apprentices, YT, etc
- Customers/guests
- Visitors and the general public

HEALTH AND SAFETY AT WORK ACT 1974

- An act to make provision for securing the health, safety and welfare of persons at work and for protecting others against the risk to health or safety arising out of activities of persons at work and for controlling use of dangerous substances.
- Every employer has a duty to ensure, as far as it is reasonably possible and practicable, a healthy safe environment for all employees.
- It is the duty of the employer to prepare and revise regularly a written statement of his/her policy on health and safety and to bring notice of said statement to his/her employees.
- It is the duty of the employee to take reasonable care for health and safety of him/herself and of other persons and to co-operate with the employer in this matter.
- No person shall intentionally or recklessly interfere with or misuse anything provided in the interests of health and safety.

The above points are of importance with reference to the Health and Safety at Work Act. There follows a list of points of safety compiled by a hospital catering manager which were included in one particular hospital's policy statement on Health and Safety. These help to illustrate the Health and Safety at Work Act in action, but please remember they are only guidelines you should always ask for specific advice from your Local Authority.

SAFETY PRACTICES — GENERAL

- All corridors, stairways and circulation areas must be kept clear of obstructions.
- Electric supply cables to equipment must not be stretched across circulation areas.
- Any liquid spilled in corridors, stairways and circulation areas must be cleaned up immediately.
- All fire exits should be clearly marked and fire escape routes indicated where necessary.
- In the event of fire, no lifts to be used.
- All machines should be fully guarded.
- Unqualified staff should not attend to any repairs of defective machinery.
- All electrical equipment should be switched off at mains supply when not in use and where possible the plug withdrawn from the socket.
- Electrical systems must not be overloaded.
- Lighting in all areas should be adequate.
- Extra care should be taken by smokers to ensure that matches, cigarettes and pipes are properly extinguished. Use ashtrays not waste paper baskets or similar receptacles.
- Great care should be exercised when lifting heavy articles and items of equipment, etc. and where necessary suitable assistance should be requested.
- Manufacturer's instructions regarding handling, storage and use of chemicals and/or other substances or articles should be strictly adhered to.
- Where supplied, protective clothing must be worn.
- Waste material should not be stored for lengthy periods but disposed of as soon as possible.
- Over-reaching or standing on chairs in order to reach a higher level must be avoided.
- Liquid soap or poisons must not be transferred into other receptacles such as soft drinks bottles which may danger the unsuspecting user.
- After using any chemicals, hands or any other parts of the body which may have been contaminated should be thoroughly washed.

SAFETY PRACTICES — FOOD AND BEVERAGE

Food and beverage personnel have a special responsibility with regard to safety as they come into contact with the general public. They must at all times be aware of the possible danger of accidents. They must also be concerned about their own safety and the safety of their fellow workers. General points include:

- Learn how to use fire-fighting equipment.
- Learn the basics of first aid.
- Walk, never run, in a restaurant.
- Concentrate on your work and do not spill food.
- Always clear well away from the table. When clearing plates turn away from the customer.
- Do not carry large quantities of china, glass or equipment. Use a tray when convenient. Load and unload trays, keeping the correct balance.
- Be aware of the space around you; do not turn around abruptly.
- Place ice buckets and stands where they will not cause obstruction.
- When offering a light to the customer, shield the flame with your hand.
- Never carry carving knives with blades pointing forwards. Place them down flat on a carving board or trolley.
- Clean carving knives after service. Never leave knives in sinks.
- Wipe wet floors straight away in service area.
- All broken china and glass should be picked up straight away and placed in a suitable container for disposal, not in a plastic bag.
- When opening bottles, especially bottles of sparkling wines, ensure the cork is not facing the customers.
- When doing flambé dishes, keep your head well away from the flame.

Handling of materials accounts for most accidents at work. The following are typical examples within a licensed establishment:
- Sometimes barrel slides or skids may be in use from the cellar hatch. Ensure that everyone stands well clear when they are in use. Special care is necessary if the slides or casks are wet.
- Block-and-tackle gantries are installed in some premises. Report any defects or indication of damage. Do not overload.
- Sometimes a full or part-full cask may require to be taken off a stillage (thrawl). This is usually a two-man job and should be done with care.
- Dump pads or dropping bags may cause accidents if they are not properly positioned, because the cask may bounce or roll the wrong way. People should stand well clear.
- Carrying boxes incorrectly can cause accidents. Never carry heaped boxes in front of you in a way that obscures your vision.
- Check the cellar before delivery and remove obstructions to the drayman.
- Handling of boxes has its dangers: there may be broken glass in the box; the edges of wooden boxes may be split and splintered or rough and jagged, if made of metal; wires may be broken on wooden boxes.
- Extreme care should be taken when carrying objects up or down stairways, e.g. kegs, crates, etc. Avoid bruised fingers and knuckles.
- Extra care should be taken when handling CO_2 cylinders having broken or split cages.

- Look out for cracked glasses when drying. Throw away all chipped and cracked glasses.
- There could be broken glass in washing-up water. Dirty glasses must not be piled in sinks so that those at the bottom get broken.
- It is possible for the rim of the bottle to break when removing the crown cork. Bottles broken in this way should be put neck first into the crate and subsequently thrown away.
- Never plunge a hand into a bottle crate; look first and so avoid seizing any broken bottles.
- Wrap up broken glass in plenty of paper before disposal.

These are obviously only a selection of possible safety guidelines, but they give us the basic idea of implementing the Health and Safety at Work Act. Your own hotel/restaurant/bar/establishment will have its own publications/posters about the HASAW Act and you should also seek advice from the Local Authority.

DUTIES OF EMPLOYERS

- Provide safe equipment and set up safe working practices.
- Provide instructions and supervision within the workplace, to ensure health and safety.
- Make sure that all materials are being used, transported and stored correctly.
- Ensure that access into and out of buildings, is easy.
- The workplace must be structurally safe, with adequate facilities such as lighting and ventilation.
- A safety policy must be drawn up and placed in such an area that it can be seen by all concerned.

DUTIES OF EMPLOYEES

- Take responsibility for your own health and safety.
- Behave responsibly, so that workmates and colleagues are not harmed by your actions.
- Carry out the safety practices laid down by your employer.
- Use all the equipment properly and do not meddle with it in such a way that it might become a danger to others.

ENVIRONMENTAL HEALTH OFFICERS

The law is enforced in most of the catering industry by Environmental Health Officers, who may enter premises at any time without warning, to carry out an inspection. If an officer is dissatisfied with any aspect, he may do any of the following:

- advise on how to correct a fault;
- issue an improvement notice to correct a fault;
- issue a prohibition notice to stop an activity which could cause serious risk;
- prosecute;
- remove or destroy items which are likely to be a serious danger.

SAFETY COMMITTEES

The HASAW Act makes everyone in the workplace responsible for safety and accident prevention, so employers and employees must work together. According to the Act, employers must work with union-appointed representatives when setting up and maintaining safety standards and procedures. There should, therefore, be a Safety Committee, or a Safety Representative to keep staff informed.

HAZARD PREVENTION

Safety at work is a joint responsibility, shared with employer and employees. Accidents don't 'just happen', they are caused and therefore preventable. Three main factors corporate to produce accidents:

- Technical equipment (e.g. ineffective guards on machinery)
- Working environment (e.g. noise, preventing warnings from being heard)
- Workers (e.g. inappropriate humour)

Ultimately, all accidents come down to **human failings**. People make mistakes: the architect may have made design mistakes; the contractors, installation mistakes; the worker, mistakes in procedures. Various theories have been advanced to explain the causes of accidents, such as 'pure chance', where accidents are thought to be acts of God; or 'accident-prone worker' where some people will inevitably have more accidents than others because of personal characteristics. These fatalistic 'reasons' may be dismissed as excuses rather than rational attempts to find a cause.

In Britain, one year's analysis of accidents in factories showed that injuries occurred as follows: 30% from handling goods; 16% from falls, and 14% from machinery. These figures are comparable to those for other workplaces and show the mundane nature of most accidents.

Hazard spotting should be an ongoing procedure that all members of staff should take responsibility for. Staff should know to whom they should report hazards. This would usually be their supervisor. The supervisor must then act on this information. Most establishments will have a proper procedure for dealing with hazards. Large establishments will have a Safety Committee that will meet at regular intervals to control and rectify any problems that may affect the safety of employees and guests. Written records should be maintained in order to ensure all reported hazards have been rectified. Safety Committee members may also be responsible for carrying out random hazard-spotting checks.

The following information gives advice and guidelines on some of the most hazardous situations concerning electricity in the workplace. Please remember always to contact your Local Authority for **specific advice** relating to your own workplace.

ELECTRICITY AND ELECTRICAL EQUIPMENT

Everything to do with electricity should be treated with care and respect. Equipment should only be used:

- according to the manufacturer's guidelines;
- in accordance with Health and Safety legislation;
- after the operator has been fully trained.

Safety signs should be displayed immediately adjacent to large items of equipment, e.g. food mixers. The main cause of electric shock in licensed premises are:
- defective earthing of electrical equipment;
- damaged cables, flexes, plugs and sockets;
- overloading of circuits and fuses;
- faulty electrically-operated machinery, e.g. beer pumps, sump pumps, cooling equipment, etc. in cellars and bars;
- faulty electrically operated equipment, e.g. heaters, coolers, TVs, washing machines, etc. in public and domestic parts of premises.

Electrical equipment is normally quite safe, providing it is installed properly and regularly inspected, but when accidents do occur they are usually due to careless and thoughtless actions.

❖ **Always remember that water and liquids are conductors of electricity and their association with any of the above faults would make the shock more severe.**

Safety precautions
- **Never** touch electrical equipment with wet hands.
- **Never** move any portable electrical equipment without disconnecting it from the mains.
- **Always** keep electric supply cables and pumps away from wet floors.
- **Never** allow cables to remain in a position where they can be damaged by being walked over or knocked when goods are being moved about.
- **Always** disconnect cellar pumps from the mains supply before servicing them.
- **Always** switch off all equipment except coolers, when not required, especially during non-trading hours. TV sets and amplifiers should be disconnected at night by removing the plug from the socket.
- **Do not** use portable hand inspection lamps unless they are connected to a low voltage supply and properly earthed.
- Low voltage supply must be used for counter mountings or display material in the bar area. **Never** use mains voltage.
- **Do not** clean any form of lighting or shade without first switching off the electricity supply.
- **Always** switch off portable electric beer pumps in cellars before washing down the floors. Such pumps should be on stands clear of the floor, or mounted on the wall.
- **Always** keep fuse boxes closed.
- **Always** switch off the supply to any item of equipment which requires renewal of the fuse, and use the **correct** rating of fuse for replacement. Further failures must be notified to the owner for checking into defects in the installation.

- Two-way, three-way or multi-electrical plug adaptors must not be used in any part of licensed premises.
- A placard of 'Electrical Shock Treatment' should be prominently displayed in all cellars where electrical equipment is in use.

❖ **Remember: only qualified electricians should undertake the installation, repair, or extension of mains voltage wiring.**

Safety checklist example for using electrical equipment

- Check to make sure that all equipment is in good, safe working order. Check plugs, flex, sockets.
- Remember to place plug in socket before you switch on. Never use electrical equipment with wet hands.
- Never use faulty equipment. Report at once. Make sure that no-one else uses it.
- If electrical equipment is faulty, or if it stops, switch off and remove plug before checking.
- Never use electrical equipment near water.
- Keep hands away from all moving parts, and always use safety guard.
- Follow instructions for use very carefully.
- Make sure equipment is serviced regularly.
- When you finish, switch off and unplug before cleaning well.
- Check equipment after cleaning.

ELEMENT G1.4   *Maintain a safe environment for customers, staff and visitors*

Identify ten potential hazards where you work and note how you ensure they are not dangerous.

1 ....

2 ....

3 ....

4 ....

5 ....

6 ....

7 ....

8 ....

9 ....

10 ....

ELEMENT G1.5 *Maintain a secure environment for customers, staff and visitors*

1 List the areas at your place of work which have to be kept locked.

....

....

....

2 Where are the keys or who has the keys?

....

3 List the places in your work where customers are **not** allowed.

....

....

....

4 What is the procedure for dealing with lost property?

....

....

....

5 What should you do if you find a person whom you don't know in a staff only area?

....

....

Record of Achievement – Completion of Unit G1

Candidate's signature ....

Assessor's signature ....

Date ....

MAINTAIN A PROFESSIONAL AND HYGIENIC

APPEARANCE

Personal hygiene

People who handle food must have very high standards of personal cleanliness to ensure that they do not contaminate food. In fact, if they don't, they are actually breaking the law. Government Health Inspectors carry out regular checks on premises such as factories and restaurants where food is prepared. If they feel that hygiene standards are not high enough they will prosecute.

There are ten rules for personal hygiene that should always be followed by anyone working with food:

- Wash your hands thoroughly before starting work, after handling raw foods, between handling different foods, and after visiting the toilet.
- Keep fingernails short and clean and don't bite them when handling foods.
- Cover cuts with a waterproof dressing (usually blue).
- Do not wear jewellery, rings or watches when working with food.
- Do not smoke in food areas.
- Do not cough or sneeze over food.

- Do not brush your hair or put on make-up in a food room.
- Avoid unhygienic habits: do not lick your fingers, pick your nose, ears or teeth, scratch your hair, spots or bottom. All these habits transfer bacteria to your hands and so to food.
- Wash thoroughly or bath daily.
- Always wear protective clothing including headgear.

Staff standards of hygiene are an indication of the standard of hygiene throughout the establishment. An immaculate member of staff will convince the customer that everything else is equally clean and fresh. Particularly noticeable are:

- hair – this should be clean and off the face;
- personal freshness – danger points are breath, underarms and feet;
- hands and fingernails – these should be clean with no nail biting, no nail varnish, and no nicotine stains.

These points are things which you need to consider; the neglect of any of these areas could put you in a position where you are 'fifteen love' down before you have had a chance to communicate with the customer. First impressions are very important. Apart from the areas listed above, ask yourself the following questions:

- Moustaches: Are they acceptable?
- Clothing: Is it clean and pressed?
- Shoes: Are they clean?
- Jewellery: Are you wearing too much?

You will not get a second chance of making a first impression. Any of the above which are out of place are likely to affect your relationship with the customer. Remember also to smile – it works wonders. Approach the customer; do not stand still. Finally, practise looking the customer in the eye. People buy people; confidence in oneself and one's approach will be identified by the customer and will work in your favour.

UNIFORMS

Uniforms should not be worn to and from work, as they may be contaminated in areas where hygiene standards are lower than those found in the food service area, e.g. on buses. Such contamination would then be transferred to crockery, to food and finally to mouth!

Uniforms must be clean and changed regularly. The wearing of uniform identifies your occupation. It helps to give a good impression of the establishment or company. It should be well designed, well fitting and in good condition.

- Always be smart on arriving for duty.
- Never appear in public areas unless in full uniform.
- Dress in changing room, never in the restaurant/bar area.
- Uniform must be spotlessly clean and freshly laundered at all times and in good repair.

INFECTIOUS DISEASES

There are many infectious diseases and most people will suffer from one of them at one time or another. Remember that a food handler suffering from an infectious disease could pass it on by way of food to other people. If a food handler has an infectious disease, he/she should inform the supervisor.

Also, if a food handler has been in contact with someone with an infectious disease, she/he should report it. Some people are carriers of a disease. This means that although they don't feel ill themselves, they can pass on the disease to others. This is especially dangerous in the food industry.

Think of a restaurant that you have eaten in recently. In the space below make some notes about its standards of hygiene.

....

....

....

....

....

❖ **Food handlers have a special responsibility to make sure they do not pass disease on to others.**

DISEASES ASSOCIATED WITH FOOD

The most serious diseases commonly associated with food are dysentery and diarrhoea, and food poisoning.

Dysentery and diarrhoea

These are severe gastrointestinal upsets spread by poor personal hygiene. They are most common in schools and other institutions where large numbers of people share the same toilets.

Food poisoning

Food poisoning is caused by eating food infected with bacteria. This brings about gastrointestinal upsets, characterised by vomiting and diarrhoea, within a few hours of eating.

❖ **Remember**

Personal hygiene is especially important to food service staff because:

1 Staff will be serving food.

2 They will have close contact with customers.
3 You may be the first representative of the management the guest meets when entering the restaurant. Your attitude and appearance influence the impression the guest gets. A first impression very often determines the total impression.
4 First impressions should be one of welcome.
5 The first priority should be to gain the customers' confidence when they come into the restaurant/bar.

ROLE OF SUPERVISORY STAFF

You may represent the management in customer contact. On you and your staff rests the main task of selling to and satisfying the guest.

The following example of a customer care checklist may be used by supervisors to train and assess food service staff.

1 Good clean fresh appearance ☐
2 Clean teeth, fresh breath ☐
3 Hands: clean ☐
4 Fingernails: kept short, no nail varnish, clean and well manicured ☐
5 Hair: clean, neat, well groomed ☐
6 Clean shaven face or clean well trimmed beard or moustache ☐
7 Jewellery, make-up, perfume or aftershave only in moderation ☐
8 No unpleasant personal habits (smoking, nail biting) ☐
9 Uniform worn correctly, clean, well pressed, and a good comfortable fit ☐
10 Shoes worn correctly, safe, comfortable, clean and in good repair ☐
11 Works hygienically ☐
12 Washes hands regularly ☐
13 Covers minor cuts, burns, abrasions with clean waterproof dressing, changed regularly ☐
14 Reports any hygiene hazards ☐

Environmental/Food service hygiene

Food service personnel may handle a variety of foods and equipment. Incorrect handling may cause the customer harm. Some aspects of environmental hygiene are the responsibility of the employer. Employers must supply staff with:

- adequate changing facilities;
- adequate toilet facilities;
- adequate handwash basins with soap, nail brush and hand-drying facilities;
- first aid facilities;
- training on aspects of personal and environmental hygiene.

Employees must ensure they carry out their work in a hygienic manner – failure to do so often results in disciplinary procedures and can result in legal action.

A thorough understanding of all the dos and don'ts of food handling is essential.

This understanding will only be the result of good training.

We will now examine specific hygiene practices which should be employed within the food service establishment.

EQUIPMENT

Glasses

Prior to any food service activity, glasses need to be polished, with a clean, dry glass cloth, to ensure that they are dust- and germ-free. If they are left for a period of time, dust particles and air-borne bacteria may collect either on or in the glass. They should be handled as little as possible and when necessary by the stem only. To avoid a build up of dust particles they should be placed upside down on the table until the commencement of service.

Glasses used for bar service should be stored upside down and need to be washed and polished regularly even if they are not all used each day. If regular washing does not take place, a particularly busy opening period will result in beverages being served in dusty, contaminated glasses. Glasses should be washed either by a machine designed for that purpose or in a sink available for that function only. When glasses are washed by machine, it is essential that the following points are observed:

- the water temperature is correct;
- the detergent container is adequately filled with glass detergent;
- the water jets and the inside of the washer are cleaned regularly;
- glasses are examined for lipstick and if necessary washed again;
- glasses are air-dried and finally polished with a clean, dry cloth;
- the washer is used solely for glass washing;
- if glasses persistently fall below standard, the machine is serviced.

If glasses are hand washed, the following points should be observed:
- water will require to be changed at regular intervals depending upon usage;
- glasses are rinsed after washing;
- glasses are examined for lipstick and if necessary washed again;
- glasses are air-dried and finally polished with a clean, dry cloth.

Inadequately cleaned glasses not only harbour germs but also detract from the taste and bouquet of the beverage served in them.

Crockery

Ask yourself these two questions:
- Have you ever been offered a dirty plate in a restaurant?
- What are your lasting impressions of that establishment?

The chances are that a dirty plate offered in a restaurant will make a lasting impression regardless of the quality of the food. It is imperative that we pay particular attention to crockery as it plays not only a practical role but an aesthetic one as well. It is a significant part of the 'meal experience'. Let us look at some simple rules to follow:

- The handling of crockery should be kept to a minimum. Use a service cloth: hands help to pass bacteria and germs from you to the crockery to the customer.
- Use a clean service cloth for each food service session.
- Never use cracked or chipped crockery – they provide the ideal environment in which bacteria will multiply.
- Always polish crockery with a clean dry cloth before presenting it at the table.
- Always wash crockery after use even if it has only been used as an underplate for pepper and salt – it will have been touched and although it may look clean it could harbour bacteria.
- Never leave dirty crockery in the stillroom between sessions. Always wash all crockery before the completion of the service – bacteria will multiply on plates left in a warm kitchen between services.
- Always clear crockery of food debris before washing.
- Always store crockery in a clean and preferably separate area.
- Never take chances even when under pressure – one chance is one too many.

The washing of crockery requires special consideration; when a machine is used you must ensure that:
- there is a supply of detergent to the machine;
- the water jets are not blocked;
- the filter trays are clean;
- the machine is emptied and refilled at regular intervals;
- the water is at correct temperature;
- crockery is allowed to air dry after washing;
- regular servicing of the machine takes place.

If crockery persistently falls below standard when the above points have been acted upon then the machine may require professional servicing.

Cutlery

Cutlery may be either stainless steel or silver-plated. Both must be perfectly clean and handling should be kept to a minimum. When cutlery is handled it must be with a clean service cloth thus avoiding contact with the hands and limiting the risk of contamination.

All cutlery items must be washed correctly after use by a dishwasher through which they should be passed upright in containers and not flat as washing would be ineffective. Forks, particularly those used for breakfast service, may require prewashing as egg protein is liable to stick to cutlery.

Cutlery should always be polished with a clean cloth to avoid smears. In the case of silver-plated cutlery, silver polishing is required regularly by using silver dip, silver polish or a burnishing machine. These methods involve the use of toxic solvents and this activity should take place in an area away from food and other restaurant equipment. Following polishing, silver plated cutlery must be washed. These remarks apply also to other silverware.

Coffee machine/butter machine

Both must be thoroughly cleaned after use. The water used in the making of all beverages must be freshly drawn from the mains, otherwise there is a risk of contamination and a stale taste will be imparted.

STORAGE AREAS

Fridges

The cleaning of refrigerators has already been mentioned. It is particularly important that food, particularly dairy items, be kept no longer than their shelf life and that all items are covered. In the case of butter which has been in the restaurant at room temperature it should not be re-used in the restaurant but passed on for use in cooking.

Bain-maries

When food is stored in a bain-marie or other hot storage unit it should be maintained at a temperature above 70°C and covered where possible. Hot foods should only be stored over the service period.

Cold food and displayed food

In the case of cold foods, these should be stored under refrigeration and covered where possible. In cases where food is displayed, all storage areas must be thoroughly cleaned after each service.

Refuse

A separate area for the storage of refuse should be available. Food debris should not be allowed to build up in the food service or stillroom area. This can be achieved by ensuring that plates containing debris are cleaned from the table after each course and taken directly to the dishwash area. Refuse from the dishwash area must be removed at the end of each service to prevent bacteria multiplying and cross-contamination occurring.

Similar consideration should be paid to room service, stillroom and bar areas. Food debris should be kept separate from other waste.

Dry store

Where coffee, sugar, tea, cereals, etc. are stored, each should be in a separate sealed container and the storage area must be cleaned regularly.

RESTAURANT/BAR

Any build-up of dust in the restaurant will lead to a build-up of bacteria and increase opportunities for that bacteria to be transferred to crockery or food, thus increasing the risk of contamination. It is also possible for food to 'hide' under tables, sideboards, carpet edges, etc., thus inviting vermin and contamination. Restaurant hygiene standards can be maintained if:

- the carpet is vacuumed regularly prior to the lay-up of tables for each service in order to remove food debris and dust particles that may be brought in from outside;
- carpets are cleaned regularly;
- dusting takes place each day;
- air conditioning replaces air at regular intervals;
- dogs or other animals are never allowed to enter;
- curtains, chairs, tables, woodwork, lights and service stations are cleaned regularly and moved where possible;
- counters, trolleys, etc. used to store food, are cleaned after each service;
- tables are wiped with a clean cloth, or tablecloths and serviettes changed after each guest has left.

BUFFETS AND CARVERIES

Bacteria will grow and multiply rapidly if food is maintained within the temperature range 5 to 63°C centigrade. The risk of contamination is further increased if food is stored within this temperature range for any length of time. Buffets and carveries provide ideal conditions for bacteria unless correct hygiene practices are applied. It is essential therefore, that the following rules are followed:

- Cold food where possible should be stored below 5°C when displayed at the point of sale.
- Food to be served hot should be maintained above 63°C when displayed for sale.
- All food should be covered where possible.
- Food items, once displayed, should not be allowed to cool and then reheated prior to a second display.

Where the first two points cannot be achieved, food items should be taken directly from the food preparation area (where correct storage conditions prevail) to the service point at the latest possible moment and left for as short a time as practicable.

ELEMENT G2.1   *Maintain a professional and hygienic appearance*

1   Give five reasons why it is essential to wear appropriate clean smart clothing.

a) ....

b) ....

c) ....

d) ....

e) ....

2   What is the uniform you are required to wear at work?

....

....

3   Why must all hair be kept clean and tidy?

....

....

4   What is meant by personal hygiene?

....

....

....

5   Why should jewellery not be worn?

....

....

6   What are the company rules relating to make-up?

....

....

7   It is possible for food to 'hide' under tables, sideboards, carpet edges, etc. List eight restaurant hygiene standard checks which should be carried out after each service.

a) ....

b) ....

c) ....

d) ....

e) ....

f) ....

g) ....

h) ....

Record of Achievement – Completion of Unit G2

Candidate's signature   ....

Assessor's signature   ....

Date   ....

Unit G3

DEAL WITH CUSTOMERS

Customer care

SOCIAL SKILLS AND 'YOUR CUSTOMER'

In order to attract the customer to come to the restaurant and to return involves pleasing the customer, which is a 'tall order', as all customers are different with varying interests, ideas and demands. This requires the waiting staff to act in a public relations role.

Social skills are the personal skills developed by staff which create a relationship with the customer. Relationships with your customers are very important and are a result of personal reaction between yourself and the customer. They are also developed by what we do, which greatly affects and influences your customer's satisfaction. Social skills make a guest feel at home in a friendly and relaxed atmosphere. Thus, the success of the restaurant depends upon the waiting staff's relationship with the customer.

❖ **It is important to be a real host to your guests and make them feel at home.**

FIRST IMPRESSIONS

Telephone enquiry

Usually the first impression the customer gets of the restaurant occurs before you actually meet, when you answer the telephone. It is most important to greet the customer, giving the restaurant's name, your own name, and asking how you may help. Be attentive to their needs and requests, be professional, record all the details in the bookings diary. Repeat confirmation to the customer. At the end of the conversation say 'Thank you for your booking, we shall look forward to seeing you'.

Establishment

The appearance of the establishment both inside and out provides the potential customer with an impression. Well designed, clean premises will help to create a good impression and sell the restaurant. Once inside, the customer will be further influenced by the decor, layout, design and atmosphere.

Restaurant

The restaurant is the shop window for all the hard work that goes into a smooth-running food operation. The customer buys not only food and drink, but a complete package – the dining experience. The customer's first impression should be one of welcome, readiness and order. A sense of pleasurable anticipation should be created. This requires detailed planning for all aspects of service.

Staff

The personal appearance of staff is of paramount importance to create a good first impression: how you look, are dressed, groomed, walk and appear to the customer. Someone who looks good, feels good and is confident, in turn makes the customer confident. Your appearance helps to sell an establishment's service and food, and you yourself.

Appearance is very important in communication. If someone does not like what they see, your verbal message probably won't be listened to or acted upon. First impressions count a great deal to guests and to your employer. No potential customer expects to be met by a carelessly dressed individual with an unwelcoming attitude. It is important that you reflect the operation in which you work, and the product, service and company you represent.

❖ **Remember first impressions are lasting.**

BODY LANGUAGE AND COMMUNICATION

Are you aware that only a small percentage of the impression you make on other people is a result of speaking to them? What has a greater impact on them are **non-verbal messages**. These include all forms of communication other than actual words:

- Vocal pitch and emphasis
- Speed of speech
- Breathing
- Posture/stance
- Facial expression
- Eye contact
- Eye movements

- Pupil size
- Distance from others
- Gestures
- Clothing/dress
- Choice of words/jargon
- Handshake

No wonder body language is described as the language we all speak, but very few understand. To establish the significance of non-verbal communication, imagine you are meeting someone for the first time. Consider how much you make an impression on others by the actual words you say; the way you speak; your body language.

Analysis has shown that you make a greater impression on others by the use of body language. Body language is the message you receive when you watch a silent film. Body language tells you more about what people really mean than all the words in the world. Many gestures and signals are communicated without us consciously realising it. Very small ordinary gestures that usually go unnoticed, are important.

Actors represent a good example of body language: the words they use are often the same, but whether they are good or bad in the role, succeed or not, depends entirely on their body language skills and the degree to which their words and body language convey the same message. Words may lie, but the body seldom does.

By interpreting other peoples' body language you can ascertain if the people you are communicating with are sympathetic or bored. You can decide whether they are open, nervous, angry or worried. The importance of this to people in a service situation is obvious.

When reading body language, you cannot just look at one detail and draw conclusions from it. In order to get a reasonably good picture of a person's thoughts and feelings from their body language, you should try to assess the body signals as a whole and see them in the context of the situation. In order to be reasonably accurate, at least three signals should be giving the same message.

Never forget that while you are reading the body language of customers, they are also reading yours. You are constantly being judged by your face, voice and your body language. If, for example, you raise your shoulders, lower your head, seem impatient, speak with a tired, bored or irritated voice, the customer could think:

- you don't like your work;
- you are stressed;
- you are not in control of the situation;
- you are not friendly;
- you don't show respect for other people;
- you do not want to help, and when you do help, you do so unwillingly.

THE FIRST MEETING — WELCOMING THE GUEST

The **welcome** is the first meeting and therefore very important. We use the word welcome as this is the key word in customer relations: we want to welcome the customer and make him/her feel welcome. Welcoming guests is often overlooked. People just drift into the restaurant instead of being met by a smiling member of staff. A few phrases of pleasant conversation after a sincere 'Good evening Sir/Madam', can help to relax and unwind even the most nervous visitor. If the customer is a regular then they should be addressed by name when first greeted.

Translate the menu in detail. This is a wonderful opportunity to:

- establish a good relationship with the customer;
- use your selling skills to promote speciality dishes and wines.

This requires knowledge of the menu, a pleasant manner and enthusiasm about the product. To sell a product effectively, you have to believe in it, have pride in your work and the establishment. In addition to serving skills you need to cultivate personal qualities to become an effective restaurant sales person.

It is most important to establish a good relationship with the customer from the start. Listen carefully to what the customer says. Spending time with your customer is worthwhile. Assure them they are going to enjoy their meal/evening.

❖ **Remember**

1   Customers, who feel a bond with you, don't complain they ask.
2   A pleasant welcome can gain a sale.

3   A poor welcome loses the sale.

CONVERSING WITH CUSTOMERS

Conversing with the customers helps to create and maintain a good warm friendly atmosphere:

- A courteous friendly approach to guests need not involve unnecessary chat.
- Staff should converse with customer and non-commercial topics.
- If a customer enters into conversation with you, answer politely, but briefly, and tactfully excuse yourself at the first opportunity.
- Never discuss other guests with customers, nor give information regarding guests.
- Do not listen to guests' conversation.
- Never use bad language.

Speech

Friendliness towards the customer is most important, but you must always be courteous. Exaggerated friendliness or familiarity is seldom appreciated. Service staff are constantly 'on show', but try to be as unobtrusive as possible.

Speak in a clear voice, pitch your voice low, and pronounce words precisely. Speak in good English. Customers like to hear a clear pleasing voice, so do not speak quickly. Knowledge of a second language is helpful, particularly when serving tourists.

PERSONAL SERVICE/PERSONAL SKILLS OF FOOD SERVICE

The aim of good social skills is to please the customer. Some customers eat out not just to satisfy hunger, but for change, amusement, to see and be seen – in other words, for entertainment. Staff add value to the meal experience. Personal service forms a bond with the customer which you develop and maintain during service and departure. This stays with the customer who will book again, i.e. repeat business.

Restaurant service is a skilled and responsible job; food service staff have to be sales people, diplomats and negotiators. Some of the qualities and skills involved in personal service are as follows:

- Ability to communicate well
- Good listening skills
- Identification of particular customer needs
- Customer knowledge
- Attentiveness
- Ability to converse knowledgeably on the menu and topics related to the meal
- Knowledge of company policy

❖ **It is important to remember that satisfied customers are your most effective sales force.**

Customer care checklist

The following example of a customer care checklist may be used by supervisors to train and assess food service staff.

Customer relations

1 Greets the customer warmly, politely with a smile, the host is identified by name if known ☐
2 Speech is clear and precise ☐
3 Customer seated with minimum fuss ☐
4 Helpful and attentive to customer ☐
5 Listens carefully to customer ☐
6 Positive, confident manner ☐
7 Attends to customer's special needs ☐
8 Uses initiative ☐
9 Has good body language ☐
10 Meets customer's needs ☐
11 Works well as part of the team ☐
12 Good attitude ☐
13 Copes well with pressure ☐

Taking customer's order
1 Menu presented to customer, promptly ☐
2 Clear and helpful advice given to customer on menu and content of dishes ☐
3 Change of cover made dependent on customer's order ☐

Service of meal
1 Food served to customer with minimum disturbance to customer ☐
2 Food is served at correct temperature ☐
3 Food is attractively presented to customer ☐
4 Takes pride in good presentation ☐

Departure
1 Customer assisted with coats ☐
2 Word of thanks, 'hope you enjoyed your meal' ☐
3 Good day/night, 'we look forward to seeing you again' ☐

ELEMENT G3.1 *Maintain customer care*

1 Why is it important to be polite to customers on arrival as well as departure?

....

....

....

....

....

2 How can you identify a customer's needs in a restaurant situation?

....

....

....

....

....

3   List items that help you to establish and/or anticipate what a customer might require.

....

....

....

....

....

4   The customer is liable to ask you many questions about the establishment. Make a list of the services that you are aware of. These may cover such items as meal times, room service, morning call sheet, and various local amenities.

....

....

....

....

....

5   Obtain evidence of the various services that are available to your customers.

....

....

....

....

....

....

6 What are the procedures for handling customers' comments?

....

....

....

....

....

7 Does your establishment have any special features that favour customers who are
   disadvantaged through immobility, sight impaired or hard of hearing?

....

....

....

....

....

8 Does your establishment have an area set aside for children? If not would this help
   in developing further trade?

....

....

....

....

....

Handling complaints

Complaints may be made informally or formally. Those made informally may arise from service personnel detecting through body language or speech that all is not well. Complaints of this nature if detected early should be the easiest to deal with. There are seven basic steps:

- Welcome the complaint, thank the guest for bringing it to your attention.
- Express regret, but do not admit that you or your establishment is to blame.
- Listen attentively, do not interrupt the customer even if you know the complaint may have to be dealt with by another person.
- Collect the facts.
- Offer to consider her/his suggestion and act, this will depend on company policy.
- Make sure the customer is kept informed.
- Prevent any further complaints, both from that customer or other customers complaining about the same problem.

Some establishments have a system of completing a workplace complaints form stating the nature of the complaint and the action taken to resolve it.

Complaints made in a more formal manner may include a letter written to a member of management. These are usually of a more serious nature and require a careful investigation of the facts prior to action being taken. This will depend on the customer care policy of the organisation and perhaps on trading legislation if legal action is a possibility.

Members of staff should be aware of their specific responsibility and options available to them whilst handling any complaint. They should also be aware of when and to whom relevant information should be passed on. Complaints may relate to:

- products
- services
- environment
- personnel

❖ **Dealing well with a complaint will almost certainly win a loyal customer. A complaint is an opportunity to turn customer dissatisfaction into customer satisfaction.**

❖ **Remember**

1. All customers should be treated as VIPs.
2. Customers may be wrong, but never let them feel they are.
3. Many customers are nervous and unsure; they need help and reassurance.
4. Customers often want advice: give it.
5. Observe customers carefully; body language tells you a lot – when they need attention, when they don't.
6. There should always be someone in charge.

7   Identify customer expectations.
8   Staff are there to meet and satisfy customer demands.

❖ **The customer buys not only food and drink, but a complete package – 'the dining experience'. The most important point to remember is in everything you do and say, stop and think 'Would I be happy if I was the customer?' The aim is customer care.**

<u>ELEMENT G3.2</u>   *Deal with customer complaints*

1   What is your establishment's procedures in dealing with complaints received from customers?

....

....

....

....

....

2   List the important reasons for dealing with complaints promptly.

....

....

....

....

....

....

....

3 Why is 'listening to the customer' almost as important as being able to deal with the complaint?

....

....

....

....

....

4 If you are not in a position to deal with a particular complaint, who do you report to?

....

....

....

....

....

5 Why is it so important to relate the complaint to the most senior person present?

....

....

....

....

....

6   What is liable to happen to complaints that are not dealt with speedily and efficiently?

....

....

....

....

....

ELEMENT G3.3   *Deal with customer incidents*

1   Even in the best run establishments minor accidents will happen. What procedures does your establishment have when dealing with the following?

Spillages of food ....

....

....

Spillages of water, beverages, sauces ....

....

....

These can happen to the customer and to the table at which the customer is sitting. Explain how these are dealt with.

....

....

....

....

....

2   Breakages of equipment and particularly glassware can be most dangerous. How
    have you been trained to deal with them?

    ....

    ....

    ....

    ....

3   Customers can misplace belongings quite readily and can become most upset when
    a particular item goes missing. How would you deal with this situation? What
    procedures have been laid down to deal with these situations?

    ....

    ....

    ....

    ....

    ....

    ....

    ....

4   In a large establishment children who are left unattended, and especially when
    there are a number of them, can become 'lost'. How would you deal with a lost
    child or children?

    ....

    ....

    ....

    ....

5 What incident or accident must be reported immediately to a superior?

....

....

....

....

6 What laid down procedures does your establishment have when dealing with lost property?

....

....

....

....

Record of Achievement – Completion of Unit G3

Candidate's signature   ....

Assessor's signature   ....

Date   ....

Unit G4

OPERATE A PAYMENT POINT AND PROCESS
PAYMENTS

Till procedures

In this section we will look at the practices and procedures for handling UK and foreign cash and cash equivalents.

FLOAT PROCEDURE

Prior to service, it is important for a designated person to collect the 'float' from the cashier. This may take the form of bags and notes which have to be put into the appropriate section of the till drawer, or it may be a complete drawer insert with the money already positioned. In either case, the person receiving the float must sign to say that they have received it. The amount of money in the float will be standardised by the company and will be the same amount each time. The use of the standard float statement should be encouraged. This means that each time the float is used the same form will be used. This allows for continuity and added security, as each member of staff will use the same form at all times.

Before putting the money into the till, it should be checked carefully. This is best done with another person in attendance to act as a double check and for security reasons. All the coins and the notes should be counted. If the float is in bags, the money will have to be put into the sections in the drawer. This is done by putting the coins of the smallest denominations into the sections starting at the right hand side and progressing to the left as the value of the coins increases. The same procedure applies to the positioning of notes and the sections: the smallest denominations at the right moving to the left as the value of the notes increases.

The above method applies in general; but if there will be only one person operating the till and that person is left-handed, the entire procedure will be reversed, i.e. the smallest denominations will be positioned on the left.

MAINTENANCE OF EQUIPMENT

The maintenance of till equipment is very important. The correct information must be recorded and if the till is in any less than perfect working order, this may not be achieved. It is possible to have a maintenance contract. This means that a knowledgeable and experienced person will come and check over the tills periodically, about every 3–6 months. The other advantage of this is that if anything goes wrong with the till between services, the expert can be called out to mend the machine.

If the electric circuit fails, the machine may be able to be used by means of a hand crank. If this is the case, training in the correct use of this method must be given at the same time as training in the normal use of this machine. The important part of the machine which needs maintenance is the section where the information is printed on to the receipt. This may be ribbon and ink or cartridge. The keys need protection from dust and damp. This can be achieved by covering them with plastic shields. These can be easily removed for cleaning and can be replaced as necessary.

PREPARING TILL AREA FOR TRADE

Hygiene of the till area is very important, especially in the catering industry, where we are dealing with food and drink. The main thing to do is to get organised and develop a system for preparation of the area prior to service. The entire area must be clean and tidy at all times, and should be maintained during the period of work, i.e. the area around the till will be cleaned as required.

The keys of the till also require to be kept clean. If any food debris, liquid or dirt is allowed to lie on the keys, bacteria may grow. To prevent this, renewable plastic pads may be acquired. These cover the keys and protect them from dirt, etc. accumulating on them.

CHECKING THAT TILL HAS BEEN CLEARED

Before a different member of staff takes over the operation of a till, a check should be made that it has been cleared since the last operator used it. This is done by taking a reading from the till and recording the information, often on a print-out reading. This means that each person using the till starts with a clear record of transactions. It is essential that this is done, so that each period of use on the till is complete in itself and the responsibility of one person only. This may also involve a change over with new float being introduced.

RECEIPT AND AUDIT ROLLS CHANGED AS REQUIRED

Receipt rolls are those which provide the customer with a record of the amount they have spent.

Audit rolls are kept within the till. They record details of each transaction. At the end of every shift or each day's trading, the audit roll relating to that particular time is removed from the till and taken to the cashier or accounts office. The receipts in the till are married up with the audit roll and should match exactly. If this does not happen, action will have to be taken to determine why and how the discrepancy has happened.

Sometimes the audit roll and/or the till roll are only changed under supervision or by a supervisor. This is normally determined by company policy. A back-up stock of these rolls should be held by the establishment with enough kept to allow all tills to be changed once if necessary.

SECURITY PRECAUTIONS AND PROCEDURES

There are several security procedures available. These include:

- Panic button: this is a button which can be pressed by the person operating the till. This has the effect of closing the till automatically, so that no money can be taken out. Another effect of a panic button may be the setting-off of an alarm either in an area where it cannot be heard by members of the public, or the opposite, to warn customers and perhaps deter potential thieves.
- Security button: works on the same principle as the above, but also locks the door of the establishment, thereby eliminating the exit for the thieves.
- Video camera: this device records what happens in an establishment. It may be in operation all the time or it may work on a time switch recording at regular short intervals. The camera may be still or it may move around to cover more of the establishment.
- Wall-mounted mirrors: these allow for viewing of a large area of the establishment.

Whatever precautions are used in an establishment, it is important that the staff are given instructions in the correct method of use. This should be included in staff training. It is also important that staff are aware of any company policy on how to deal with a situation which involves demand for money by unauthorised person/s.

Some company policies state that in any situation all money should be handed over, believing that the safety of their personnel is more important than losing money. Other companies state that no money should be handed over, under any circumstances.

ITEMISING GOODS FOR CASH PAYMENT

- Allocate to correct department: in many establishments, products are coded, to enable a check to be kept on what articles are selling and update stock records. It is therefore important that these codes are entered in the till when goods are being 'rung up'. In some tills there is a facility for stating what the item is. The codes may be entered by use of a button on the till which will be predetermined by the company or it may be read electronically.
- Subtotalling function: the subtotalling function allows for each department total to be calculated individually. This is useful information for stock control and as a guide to popular items.

ACCEPTANCE OF LEGAL TENDER

Legal tender is any means of payment which must be accepted by law in settlement of a debt. The exact money must be given when making a purchase or the seller could refuse to accept it. A cheque can also be refused as it is not legal tender. Legal tender in the UK is listed below:

1p and 2p coins	Up to 20p
5p and 10p coins	Up to £5
20p and 50p coins	Up to £10
Bank of England £1 coins	Up to any amount

Bank of Scotland notes are not strictly legal tender; however, this does not mean that these are not used and accepted throughout the UK.

When giving customers change, a system should be developed and used. It is not enough to rely on handing over a pile of coins and notes and hoping that it is correct. The receipt should be given to the customer, then the change counted into their hand or returned on a small salver.

PRODUCT IDENTIFICATION CODES.

EPOS stands for Electronic Point of Sale terminals. These are terminals which are linked to computers or which contain their own microprocessors. After data have been put in using electronic data capture (magnetic strip or bar-code reader), they draw on stored information to calculate and process transactions and product information, and print all memory information on the till receipt/audit roll automatically.

EFTPOS stands for Electronic Funds Transfer at Point of Sale, e.g. Switch. These replicate the features of EPOS terminals but also allow the cost of goods purchased to be debited directly from customers' bank or building society accounts and credited to the retailers.

EPOS and EFTPOS are significant because they are seen as improving customer service and enable tighter stock control. This function is available in many retail outlets.

CORRECTING ERRORS

Correcting of errors can be done simply if the incorrect amount has not been processed into the till. In a case like this, there is a button which can be used to erase the error. However, if the mistake has gone into the till it is not so simple to correct. If this has happened, it is usually necessary to have a supervisor correct it. A record will be made of the error to enable the cashier to amend the records later. Company policy will dictate how this process is carried out.

ELEMENT G4.1 *Open, operate and close payment point*

1   List and describe the different types of tills and billing machines currently in use in your establishment. Differentiate between mechanical, electronic and computerised machines.

....

....

....

....

2 Collect items of paper documents that are used in operating a payment point, i.e. handover procedures, audit rolls, receipt rolls, customer bills, Pay-In slips, change/float statements, 'X' and 'Z' summaries.

3 Draw a float diagram to illustrate the laid down procedures.

4   Prepare an opening float statement for the payment point in your working area.

....

....

....

....

....

....

5   How would you give change to a person who offers payment for a Lounge bill of £4.85 with a £20 note?

....

....

....

....

....

Payment procedures

PROCEDURES AND DOCUMENTATION WHEN CASH IS COLLECTED

At the end of a day's transactions or at the end of a shift the money in the till must be given to the control office/cashier. This can be done in two ways:

- The money from the till is put into a bag and secured. The bag will have identification on it in the form of till number and the name and/or number of the member of staff who has been using the till. The money will be counted in the office either manually or by machine.
- The person who has been operating the till should extract the cash float, sort, count and total the takings and complete a cash slip.

Cash slip example

Mrs Smith operates Cash Register No.10. At the end of her period of duty she will, first of all, extract the cash float and then sort, count and total the cash takings and complete the cash slip.

The contents of the till are: 250×10p coins; 23×£1 coins; 186×20p coins; cheques from Smith £46.96, Jones £162.52; 190×2p coins; 284×1p coins; 4×£10 notes; 6×£20 notes; 33×50p coins; 58×£5 notes; 235×5p coins.

The float is £50 comprising: 1×£5 note; £10 worth of 50p pieces; £10 worth of 20p pieces; £10 worth of 10p pieces; £5 worth of 5p pieces; £1 worth of 2p pieces; £1 worth of 1p pieces.

The cash slip should appear as shown opposite:

CASHING UP AT CLOSE OF BUSINESS

It is very important to ensure that the cash and non-cash receipts in the till are accurate. This is checked by taking an 'X' reading at the start of a shift on a till and doing the same at the end of the shift. This reading on the audit roll will show how much has been rung up on the till during the shift. This total should be the same as the amount of payments taken from the customers which should be the amount of cash and non-cash in the till.

CHECKING AND RECORDING DISCREPANCIES

Any discrepancies shown up, whether over or under, must be recorded on the cash slip and signed by a supervisor.

PREPARATION OF CASH AND CHEQUES FOR BANK LODGEMENT

Preparation of cash and cheques for putting into the bank involves separating coins into different denominations and counting them into bags provided by the bank. The notes must also be separated into different denominations and counted ready to be taken to the bank. Cheques are listed by amount, cheque number and name of drawer and totalled before being taken to the bank.

NIGHT SAFE FACILITIES

Businesses which cannot pay in the bulk of their takings within banking hours can deposit the money in a night safe. A large wallet or box is issued to the customer into which he/she places the money with a pay-in slip. This is complete with a counterfoil which must be filled in with the same information.

It is sealed or locked by a supervisor or manager. The key for this container must be strictly secured at all times and for added security should not be copied, i.e. there must always only be one key in the establishment. The only other copy will be held at the bank. The wallet or box is then taken along to the night safe – a locked metal hatch in the bank wall which can be unlocked only by night safe key holders. The box or wallet is dropped in and goes down a chute into a box within the bank.

Cashing up Summary

Date:
Assistant's Name:
Register No. 14
Audit Roll Total £808.57

Daily Takings

6	x £20 notes	120.00
4	x £10 notes	40.00
57	x £5 notes	285.00
23	x £1 coins	23.00
13	x 50p coins	6.50
136	x 20p coins	27.20
150	x 10p coins	15.00
135	x 5p coins	6.75
140	x 2p coins	2.80
184	x 1p coins	1.84
	Total Cash	528.09
	Total Cheques	209.48
	Total Takings	737.57

Signatures _____

_____

Over/Under £ _____

The contents are checked by the bank staff the following day and the amount credited to the customer's account. The counter-foil, stamped by the bank staff, is then returned to the customer.

ELEMENT G4.2 *Handle and record payments*

1   How do you ascertain that a customer requires a bill?

....

....

....

....

2   How do you ascertain that the guest bill is accurate, i.e. that the correct amounts have been charged correctly, or that the appropriate codes have been used?

....

....

....

....

....

....

3   How is payment recorded, i.e. on the guest's bill, through the billing machine?

....

....

....

....

4   Draw a diagram of your cash drawer showing where each item of coin, paper note and voucher payment is held.

5   What procedure would you adopt if you had to leave the payment point?

....

....

....

....

Record of Achievement – Completion of Unit G4

Candidate's signature   ....

Assessor's signature   ....

Date   ....

Unit G5

HANDLE AND RECORD NON-CASH PAYMENTS AND
REFUNDS

Accepting cheques and credit cards

CHECKING THE CUSTOMER'S IDENTITY

Check that:
* name
* signature
* bank code

are the same as those on the cheque.

POINTS TO CHECK WHEN ACCEPTING A CHEQUE

* Date — Post-dated (forward-dated) cheques should not be taken nor stale cheques, i.e. out-of-date cheques. There is a six-month limit.
* Amount — Words and figures must be the same and any changes must be initialled. Amount should not be greater than £50/£100.
* Payee — Person to whom cheque is to be paid.
* Signature — Same as printed name on cheque. The person who is paying is known as the drawer. (The cheque is being drawn on their account.)

POINTS TO CHECK WHEN ACCEPTING A CHEQUE WITH A CHEQUE CARD

* Card — Examine the card; it must be removed from container. Retain until transaction is completed.
* Limit — £50/£100, one cheque only; per transaction up to £50/£100 is guaranteed.
* Code number — Check that the code number is the same as the code number in the top right-hand corner of the cheque.
* Card number — Payee must copy card number on to the back of the cheque.
* Expiry date — Check that the expiry date has not passed.
* Hologram — Look for changing images, e.g. £50/£100, bank symbols, words.
* Signature — Cheque must be signed in front of payee and signature must match on card and cheque. Name on the card must match printed name on cheque.

Name or your company
You are the payee

The date the cheque is issued

Code number

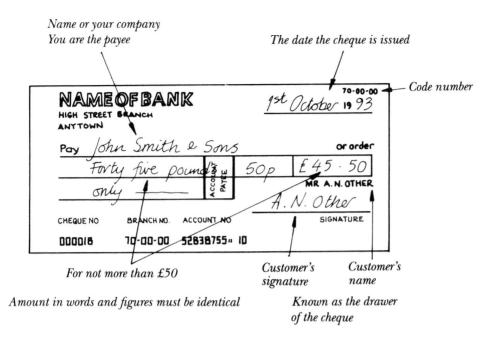

For not more than £50

Customer's signature

Customer's name

Amount in words and figures must be identical

Known as the drawer of the cheque

*Examine card
Card must be removed from wallet or container
Retain until transaction is completed*

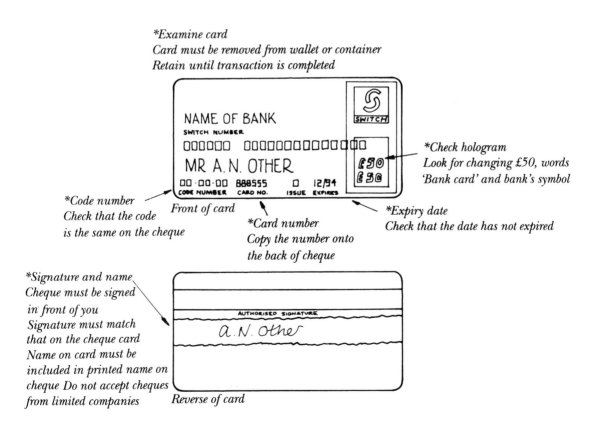

*Check hologram
Look for changing £50, words 'Bank card' and bank's symbol*

*Code number
Check that the code is the same on the cheque*

Front of card

*Card number
Copy the number onto the back of cheque*

*Expiry date
Check that the date has not expired*

*Signature and name
Cheque must be signed in front of you
Signature must match that on the cheque card
Name on card must be included in printed name on cheque Do not accept cheques from limited companies*

Reverse of card

CONDITIONS UNDER WHICH A BANK WILL GUARANTEE PAYMENT WHEN A CHEQUE CARD IS USED

The cheque must be for £50/£100 or less and has to be backed by a current cheque card which has been checked by the payee for the points detailed above. If a cheque is offered for more than the cheque card limit, company policy must be considered. It may be that it is against policy to accept cheques for more than the cheque card limit. If cheques like this are to be accepted, there are certain safeguards which can be taken:

- Extra identification should be produced, e.g. driving licence.
- Name and address should be written on the back of the cheque.
- Staff may be required to ask a supervisor to check and verify details.

However, it is worth noting that even with these extra precautions, the cheque may not be cleared by the bank. It can be a great risk to accept a cheque which does not have the backing of a cheque card. Most companies do not allow their employees to do so.

PROCEDURE TO BE ADOPTED WHEN A CHEQUE CARD IS NOT OFFERED

When a cheque card is not offered, it is important that some form of formal identification is seen. This should take the form of something printed with the customer's name on it, e.g. a driving licence. In these circumstances, a supervisor or manager should check the details.

COMPANY CHEQUES

Cheque accounts in the name of a company are not normally run with a cheque card. Another form of identification may be required to verify authenticity, e.g. letter-headed paper or a business card.

FRAUD

Cheque cards and credit cards are very easy to use and for this reason are prime targets for thieves. Because of this, lists are produced and circulated to retail outlets, of numbers of cards which have been stolen. Before any member of staff accepts a card for payment of goods and services, this list should be checked. If the card offered appears on the list, a senior member of staff should be consulted. If the signature written does not agree with the one on the card, a senior member of staff should carry out the procedures laid down by company policy.

ACCEPTANCE OF CREDIT AND CHARGE CARDS

A credit card is a way of borrowing money and is a convenient and safe method of paying for goods. Credit cards are not run by banks but by separate credit card companies. The two most common in the UK are:

- Access (generally linked with Clydesdale Bank and Royal Bank of Scotland in Scotland)
- Visa (generally linked with Bank of Scotland in Scotland)

With a credit card the customer can pay for goods and services at any place linked with the scheme. Normally signs are displayed indicating which cards are accepted. Establishments are charged by the credit card companies for using the scheme.

A statement is sent, once a month, to the customer detailing the purchases and the amount due. If the total amount is paid off monthly, then no interest charge is made; if however, only partial payment is made (a minimum amount is set down), interest will be charged on the outstanding balance.

Free credit of between 1 and 6 weeks can be obtained depending on when the card is used.

CHARGE CARDS

In addition to the above cards linked with the banks, there are several independent charge cards. The main ones are American Express and Diners Club. Basically, their use is the same as the bank cards, but they differ in one main aspect: the amount due must be fully paid every month.

IN-HOUSE CREDIT CARDS

Large stores are increasingly offering customers a credit card system to be used within their own and affiliated stores, e.g. Next, Marks and Spencers plc, John Lewis Partnership. These can be paid up each month or only the minimum paid each month. Interest will be charged on the outstanding balance.

CHECKING THE VALIDITY OF CARDS

Before use, cards must be checked for the expiry date. If the card is out of date it must not be accepted. After processing, the signature on the voucher as signed by the customer, must be checked and compared with the signature on the card. They must be the same for the transaction to be completed.

In some instances, it is necessary to have the transaction sanctioned by a manager or by a 'phone call to the head office of the credit card company. Many terminals do this automatically as the information is keyed in on a line to a computer.

Accepting foreign currency and vouchers

TRAVELLERS CHEQUES

Travellers cheques are issued by banks and some travel agents. They are cheques on the bank, paid for in advance by the customer, and are usually for fixed sums, e.g. 5, 10, 20, 50 and 100 of the relevant currency. They can also be purchased in the currency of the country which is to be visited. After buying travellers cheques, the purchaser should keep a record of all the numbers of them, separately from the cheques themselves, in case of theft.

For security reasons, the cheques must all be signed individually by the customer when purchasing them, in front of the issuing cashier. Later, when a cheque is to be cashed, it must be signed and dated in front of the person receiving it. The signatures must always be compared, and if they appear to be different, the cheque should not be cashed. These security measures are designed to ensure that no fraudulent cashing of travellers cheques is possible.

When cashing these cheques, the customer has to pay a commission; this may take the form of a percentage of the value of the cheque being cashed or it may be a fixed charge.

RATES OF EXCHANGE

Rates of exchange inform how much currency of a foreign country will be received, in exchange for 1 unit of domestic currency. In Britain, 1 unit of domestic currency is £1. Great care must be taken when identifying the country of origin in order to establish the correct rate of exchange, e.g. the difference between Canadian and US dollars. Most companies provide a list of exchange rates weekly for their units. If this is not the case, the rate should be checked with the bank as newspapers are not always reliable.

Any member of staff who may be dealing with foreign visitors, should be able to convert currencies easily. The method of conversion is simple:

To convert sterling to foreign currency
Multiply the amount by the rate of exchange:
e.g. £15 into French francs (rate £1 = 8.50 francs)
    15 × 8.50 = 127.50 francs

To convert foreign currency to sterling
Divide the amount by the rate of exchange:
e.g. 127.50 francs into sterling (rate as above)
    127.50 francs ÷ 8.50 = £15

ACCEPTANCE OF FOREIGN CURRENCY

Foreign currency refers to the money which is used in other countries. In accepting foreign currency, an establishment is undertaking a service to the customer, which is more often given by a bank. Hotels and other catering establishments charge for this service (commission). It is always charged on top of the rate for the particular currency to allow for any changes in the rates, as well as covering the charges which the bank will apply when the foreign currency is eventually paid in to them.

Foreign currency is increasingly popular as a method of payment, particularly in hotels which cater for tourists. Therefore, it is important for staff to be familiar with those currencies which are acceptable in the UK from the point of view of value and design, in order to avoid acceptance of forgeries; normally individual companies and establishments will have a list of countries whose currency is unacceptable. Banknotes from countries where exchange rates are known to fluctuate dramatically are generally regarded as unacceptable. Foreign coins of any currency are unacceptable.

ACCEPTANCE OF GIFT VOUCHERS

Gift vouchers may be given in whole or part payment for an account. These are purchased by one person, and given to another, to allow them to buy goods and services. The value of the voucher will be printed on it and this is the maximum which can be accepted. However, the total of the account may exceed the value of the voucher. In this situation, the customer will pay the excess.

The opposite situation may also occur, where the voucher exceeds the value of the account. In this circumstance, the establishment does not have to return the difference between the voucher and the account. However, establishments may decide to make it company policy that they do return this difference. This improves customer relations.

The sale of a gift voucher is recorded as such at the time of sale. When it is used to purchase goods, it is recorded as money received. In the control office the two transactions will have to be married up to avoid recording twice, the receipt of cash.

STAFF DISCOUNTS

Staff discounts must be recorded as such for control reasons, i.e. an explanation as to why less cash has been received for goods sold.

There will be a button on the till which will have to be used when recording staff discount. The level of discount may depend on the length of time of service and there may be more than one discount level. In this case there will have to be different buttons on the till.

Staff who are entitled to discount should be issued with some form of identification as proof and this should be checked by the person on the till each time a purchase is made with discount. This may take the form of company cards. These transactions will be recorded on the audit roll and will be checked by control staff each day or at the end of each shift.

REFUND PROCEDURES AND COMPANY IMAGE

The method of dealing with refunds will vary depending on company policy. It is important to be aware of your company's policy. In most instances a refund will only be authorised by a supervisor or manager. Do not offer refunds to guests without authorisation. When a guest bill is altered to reflect a refund the supervisor may sign his/her initials or complete a refund document, or hospitality docket.

Reasons for offering a refund may include:
- guest complaining about food or service;
- guests who have been overcharged or charged for an item they did not receive.

ELEMENT G5.1 *Handle and record cheque and credit/debit card payments*

1 What credit cards does your establishment accept?

....

....

....

....

2 Describe the steps you would take to authorise/validate a credit card, and a current account personal cheque?

....

....

....

....

3 What would you do if the credit card/personal cheque card was unsigned or out of date?

....

....

....

....

....

4 What special care should you take when receiving payment by a 'travellers cheque'?

....

....

....

....

5 What would you do if a guest offered a personal cheque for £20.00 in payment of a lunch bill totalling £12.75?

....

....

....

ELEMENT G5.2 *Handle and record refunds*

1 What are the procedures that you should follow when a guest requests a refund?

....

....

....

....

....

2 How would you establish the true reasons for a refund?

....

....

....

....

....

3   Describe or draw a diagram that illustrates the document that has to be completed when offering a refund.

4   How are refunds/repayments recorded and reconciled with total receipts on a pay-in slip and/or pay-in summary?

....

....

....

....

....

Record of Achievement – Completion of Unit G5

Candidate's signature   ....

Assessor's signature   ....

Date   ....

PREPARE AND CLEAR AREAS FOR TABLE SERVICE

General areas

SOUND LEVELS

It is important to reduce noise entry from outside and from the kitchen, etc. This can be achieved by using double doors from the hotplate area to the restaurant; with the use of double glazing and heavy doors, noise levels within the restaurant can be controlled. Hard wood flooring can create noise as can unlined cutlery drawers, uncovered sideboards, trolleys and tables. The greater the use of soft furnishings, the lower the noise level generated will be.

Considerable research has been undertaken by companies that sell 'canned' background music. The intention is to lighten the customer mood and determine the effect that music has on guests' feelings, conditioning them for eating and relaxing. Introducing music into a restaurant is a basic decision. The eye is not the only sense and the effect of music must be considered in depth. The selection must be in keeping with the design concept of the restaurant.

HEATING AND VENTILATION

The aim of any system is to provide a comfortable environment for the human body and different people's requirements will vary in this respect, depending on age and activity. It must be remembered that, within a restaurant, the staff will be moving around from restaurant to hotplate area, often wearing fairly warm and restrictive clothing, e.g. shirt, bow tie and jacket, whilst the guests are seated and therefore less active, and may be wearing considerably less clothing, e.g. evening dresses.

Service area

In order to create the right atmosphere in a restaurant the tasks of maintenance, cleaning and preparation must be carried out properly. The dining area must leave an impression of cleanliness and order. This cannot take place without many behind-the-scenes activities being carried out prior to service commencing.

Many of these activities are carried out in the service area between the kitchen and restaurant. This area is sometimes referred to as the stillroom. Other important ancillary services include:
* diswashing area
* hotplate area

- linen store
- silver room
- plate room

The size and use of each of these areas will vary depending on the type of establishment, e.g. hotel, restaurant, and the methods of food service carried out, e.g. plate service, silver service, carvery.

STILLROOM

In a large establishment the stillroom will provide food and drink that is not supplied by either the main kitchen or dispense bar. This usually includes hot beverages, toast, butter portions, breakfast cereals, bread, rolls, biscuits for cheese, milk and cream, preserves, condiments, sugar, fruit juice and perhaps sandwiches for afternoon teas and porridge and boiled eggs in the morning.

In the smaller establishment, the stillroom area may also hold the dishwash area and the silver and plate storage for day-to-day use.

Checklists

The following are examples of checklists which will aid the smooth running of the service area.

Dining room

Chairs dusted ☐
Tables clean ☐
Shelves/ledges dusted ☐
Sideboards dusted ☐
Glass on service doors clean ☐
All cupboards/storage areas clean/tidy ☐
Room vacuumed ☐

Bar

Shelves clean ☐
All glassware clean ☐
Bottles dusted ☐
Measures, etc. clean ☐
Till area tidy ☐
All cupboards/storage areas clean/tidy ☐
Floor swept and mopped ☐

Stillroom

Refer to next checklist

Ancillary service supervisor checklist

Staffing		Materials	
Wash-up _____		Stillroom requisition	☐
_____		Silver cleaning	☐
Stillroom _____		Refuse sacks	☐
_____			

PRE-SERVICE CHECKS

Silver room	Stillroom	Wash-up

Silver room		Stillroom		Wash-up	
Count cutlery	☐	Cruets filled	☐	**Machine**	
Clean forks	☐	Melba toast	☐	Drain plug in	☐
Other silver cleaned	☐	Butter pats	☐	Detergent on	☐
Kitchen silver order	☐	Parsley	☐	Water temperature	☐
		Sugars	☐	Plates in hotplate	☐
Burnishing machine		Special accompaniments	☐	Plate count for service	☐
Power off	☐	Coffee pots warmed	☐	Cold plates for sweets	☐
Fresh water	☐	Melba toast/rolls	☐	Coffee cups warming	☐
		Butter pats dressed	☐	Cutlery rinse	☐
				Cutlery boxes	☐
				Brock bin	☐
				Papers bin	☐

DURING SERVICE CHECKS

		Stillroom		Wash-up	
		Coffee made	☐	Brocking OK	☐
		Milk warmed	☐	Paper in bin	☐
		Checks being received	☐	Plates stacked	☐
		Fridge cleaned	☐	Clean cutlery in boxes	☐
		Stillroom cupboard cleaned	☐		

POST-SERVICE CHECKS

Silver room		Stillroom		Wash-up	
Cruets in cupboard	☐	Grill off	☐	Kitchen silver to silver room	☐
Butter dishes in cupboard	☐	Grill clean	☐	Cutlery to dummy waiter	☐
Butter knives in cupboard	☐	Coffee machine off	☐	Plates stacked	☐
Kitchen silver stacked	☐	Coffee machine clean	☐	Hotplates cleaned	☐
Cutlery counted	☐	Coffee flasks clean	☐	Machine cleaned	☐
Cutlery recorded	☐	Surfaces clean	☐	Machine washed down	☐
Cupboard locked	☐	Sinks/shelves clean	☐	Surfaces washed and dry	☐
		Floor mopped	☐	Shelves tidy	☐
		Lights off	☐	Floor washed	☐
				Lights off	☐
				Dish and net cloths	☐

Supervisor's report	Maintenance report
Supervisor's signature: _____	Day and Date: _____

Example of silver cleaning service

Day	Flatware/hollow ware	Cutlery
Monday	Soup tureens: all sizes Oval entrées: all sizes Coffee/milk jugs	
Tuesday	Silvers, round: all sizes Butter dishes Copper flare pans	Sweet spoons Sweet forks Side knives
Wednesday	Divided vegetable dishes: all sizes Vegetable lids Silver flare lamps Finger bowls	Joint knives Joint forks Teaspoons/coffee spoons Miscellaneous items, e.g. pastry slices, sugar, tongs, ladles, melba spoons, butter knives, etc.
Thursday	All cruets: salt, pepper, mustard Sugar sifters Sugar bowls All bar equipment: shakers Oil and vinegar sets	Fish knives Fish forks Hors d'oeuvre knives Hors d'oeuvre forks
Friday	Copper flare lamps Silvers, oval: all sizes Double lined timbales Sauce boats	Soup spoons Service spoons Service forks

Note: Any item that is tarnished must be cleaned during the 'Ménage'. Please pay particular attention to soup tureens, coffee/milk jugs, vegetable dishes and forks.

Duty rota

In order to ensure various tasks are fairly allocated to each member of staff a duty rota is drawn up. These tasks may also be used as a basis for staff training. A Standard of Performance List may be used to ensure company procedures are being met. This type of duty rota will vary from establishment to establishment depending on the nature of business carried out. An example of a daily duty rota is shown opposite:

Waiter/ Waitress	3 1	3 2	3 3	3 4	3 5	3 6	3 7	3 8	3 9	10	11	12	13	14	Task Number
A															Stillroom/hot plate
B															Accompaniments
C															Sideboards
D															Linen
E															Cleaning duties
F															Cleaning duties
G															Cutlery lay-up
H															Cutlery lay-up
I															Wines
J															Glassware

Restaurant area

SIDEBOARDS

Before the customers are due to arrive the sideboard should be equipped with all required items. Items commonly required to be in place for lunch and dinner service include:

- Ashtrays
- Breadbaskets
- Butter dishes
- Condiments – proprietary sauces, horseradish, etc.
- Menus
- Coffee saucers and liners
- Cruet – salt, pepper, mustards, oil and vinegar
- Cutlery – service spoons and forks, sweet spoons and forks, soup spoons, teaspoons, coffee spoons, fish knives and forks, joint knives, side knives, plus any special items, e.g. asparagus tongs
- Doyleys
- Fingerbowls
- Glassware
- Linen – extra table cloths, napkins, etc.
- Liners – for soup plates, etc.
- Checkpad and pen, or hand-held terminal

- Service cloth
- Service salver or service plate
- Side plates
- Trays
- Water jug

Service staff must ensure that their sideboards contain all the equipment that will be required during service. Silver should be sorted out into knives, forks, etc. and placed in the compartments, handles facing outward, the prongs of forks and spoons lying sideways. The order in which cutlery is placed varies according to the number of compartments but it should always be placed in the same order. One example is given below:

Service spoons and forks	Dessert spoons and forks	Soup tea and coffee spoons	Fish knives and forks	Joint knives	Side knives

CLOTHING-UP

The tablecloth is the background for an attractive lay-up and must be handled with skill to present a fresh uncreased appearance. There are three main types of cloth:
- Banquet: for long banquet or buffet tables
- Tablecloth: for small round, square or rectangular tables
- Slip cloth: for protecting larger tablecloths

In order to preserve appearance and prevent damage, linen must be handled carefully. Table linen is expensive to purchase and launder. The wrong selection means handling unwanted cloths resulting in a creased appearance.

Laying a table cloth
Stand between the table legs
Pick up the screen folds with open edges
towards you

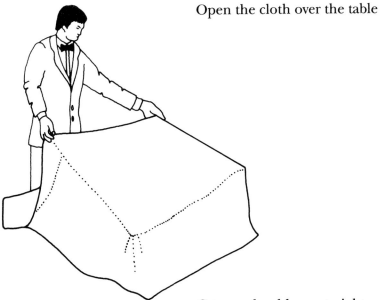

Open the cloth over the table

Creases should run straight
The overlap should be even
The corners should cover the legs
The cloth should be in good condition

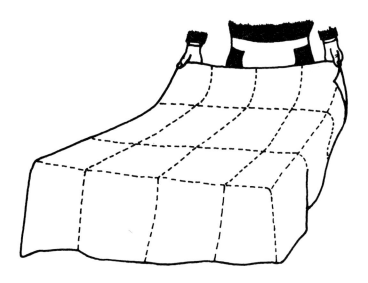

Laying a banquet cloth
Ensure cloth is long enough
One person should hold each end of the cloth
Spread folded cloth along the centre of table

Ensure creases run down centre
Ensure drop is even on both sides
Ensure cloth is in good condition

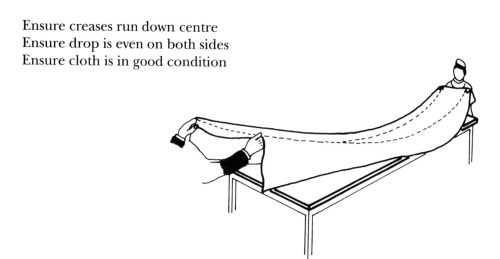

NAPKIN FOLDS

There are many napkin folds – some simple, some complex. Simple folds are used in everyday service, more complex folds are used for special events and dinners. Some establishments may use disposable napkins to reduce laundry costs; these can be purchased in a wide variety of sizes, colours and quality.

LAYING THE TABLE

Tables are laid according to house custom, which is determined by the type of menu and style of service operated. There are a variety of covers which are laid according to the type of meal and service being offered, for example:

- A la carte cover
- Table d'hôte cover
- Function cover

The diagram below shows an à la carte cover. This would be used for first-class silver service.

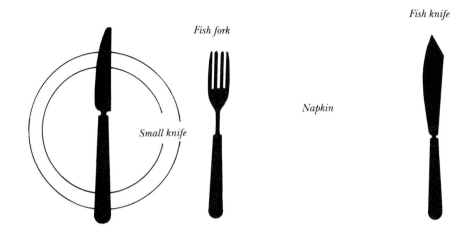

Additional items of cutlery would be placed prior to the dish being served. The diagram below shows a table d'hôte setting.

The following three diagrams are examples of function cover lay-ups. Only the cutlery that is required for the function menu will be laid.

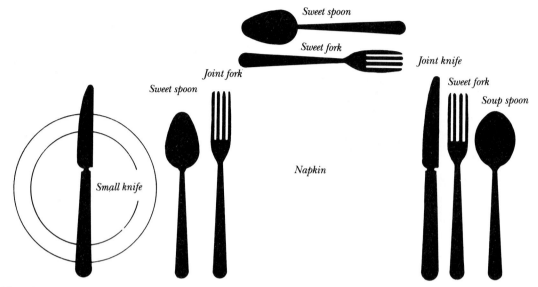

Menu: Soup, Spaghetti, Main course, Sweet

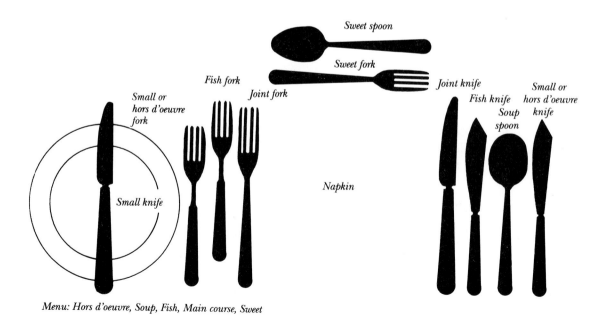

Menu: Hors d'oeuvre, Soup, Fish, Main course, Sweet

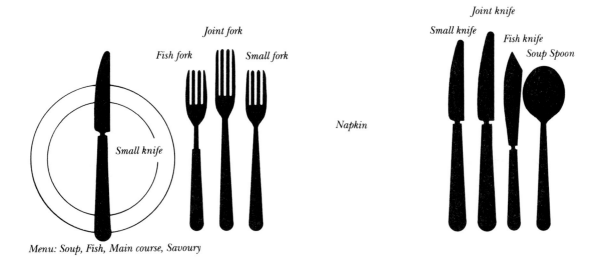

Menu: Soup, Fish, Main course, Savoury

Once cutlery has been polished ready for laying up it should be handled as little as possible.

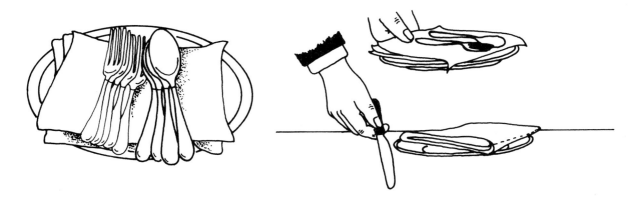

After the table d'hôte or à la carte cover has been laid, items for the centre of the table may be laid, e.g. table number, cruets, flowers, etc. Clean glassware should also be put in place, usually the top right-hand corner of the cover.

Reinstating service areas

In this section we will look at the tasks that should be carried out after servicing is complete, in some cases this means when all the guests have departed but this is not necessarily so.

Staff must be trained to ensure that this very important part of the efficient operation of the service area is not forgotten or overlooked. A checklist for both operatives and supervisors is an excellent aid to memory – it can be easy to leave out something important in the rush to complete the job.

Hotel restaurant

The meals served in a hotel restaurant are usually breakfast, lunch and dinner.

When breakfast service is finished the restaurant staff will carry out 'ménage duties'. These usually include suction cleaning, dusting of sideboards, ledges, etc., brushing and/or polishing chairs. When all these duties are complete the room will be laid-up for lunch service.

After lunch the tables must be cleared of any remaining items and relaid for dinner; linen should be changed if required.

Any perishable foods should be stored correctly: butter must be returned to the fridge; sugar must be stored in airtight containers.

After the service of dinner is complete, the restaurant will be relaid for breakfast if required. As the restaurant is usually closed for the night after the service of dinner, it is important to consider:

- Security: cupboards and storage areas should be locked.
- Safety: staff must be alert to the dangers of fire.
- Hygiene: perishables must be refrigerated; all refuse must be removed.

RESTAURANTS OPERATING 24 HOURS

Restaurants and snack bars within service areas are often open for 24 hours. This can put extra strain on staff who are always in the public eye. Cleaning has to be carried out at regular intervals; this may be done by light cleaning, e.g. of table tops, chairs, counters, etc. being done throughout the day, and more thorough cleaning being done by cordoning off sections during off-peak times, e.g. in the early hours of the morning.

Staff are usually required to carry out certain preparation tasks for the next shift coming on duty, e.g. the night staff may set up the counter area for breakfast service ensuring there is sufficient equipment and foodstuff. An understanding of the problems encountered by different 'shifts' by both supervisors and operatives is essential for the smooth running of a 24-hour establishment.

Checklist for clearing down a restaurant

Area	Duty	
Tables	All items removed	☐
	Table lamps or candles out and stored	☐
	Flowers to bar area	☐
	All glasses to bar	☐
	Coffee cups, ashtrays, etc. to stillroom	☐
Sideboards	All items cleared from sideboard	☐
	Drawers and cupboards checked	☐

Linen	All dirty linen to trolley; trolley to store	☐
	All clean linen to cupboard	☐
Bar	All glasses clean and returned to shelves	☐
	Empty bottles to crates	☐
	All equipment clean	☐
	Sinks and worktops clean	☐
	Glass wash machine empty and switched off	☐
	Rubbish to store/skip	☐
	Music system off; cupboard tidy	☐
	Floor swept and mopped	☐
Cashier	Till read; float and takings counted	☐
	Documents completed	☐
	Money and till keys to supervisor	☐

Other duties

After lunch	Carpet vacuumed	☐
	Room layout rearranged if required	☐
Safety	Hotplate off	☐
	Ashtrays and wastepaper bins emptied	☐
	All electrical equipment switched off	☐
Security	Bar area secured	☐
	All silver to cupboards	☐
	Equipment to cupboards	☐
	All cupboards locked	☐
	Windows locked	☐
	Room locked	☐

CLEARING DOWN THE SERVICE AND ANCILLARY AREAS

It is very important that after service all clearing down tasks are carried out. The stillroom and bar must be left in a state of readiness for the next service. In a hotel restaurant serving breakfast, lunch and dinner, staff usually 'set up' for the next meal and prepare as much as mise-en-place as possible.

To ensure all clearing down duties are carried out efficiently, a checklist may be used.

FAST-FOOD TAKE-AWAY

Many of the problems of continuous use encountered by the service station employees are also to be found in a fast-food operation. Many fast-food outlets are open from early in the morning until the early hours of the next morning, e.g. from 7 am until 1 am.

Night cleaners (often private contract workers) are employed to carry out many of the 'thorough cleaning' tasks required, e.g. scrubbing and buffing the floors.

Remember the three important considerations:

- Security: as the bulk of the day's takings are from evening trade, a secure system must be adopted for the storage of cash. A security firm may be employed in some areas as an extra measure.
- Safety: prior to the unit closing, a safety check must be made of the premises.
- Hygiene: many of the foodstuffs used are 'high-risk' foods and should be stored overnight at the correct temperature.

FUNCTION SUITES

When all the guests have left it is the function service staff's responsibility to clear down and reinstate the function suite. Casual staff are often employed to serve at functions and it is vital they are aware of the company policies for clearing down as these may vary from establishment to establishment.

The type of function and type and size of function suite is also important, so too are the requirements for the following day. The banqueting head waiter/waitress or banqueting manager should be aware of the exact requirements for any following function – usually via the Function Day Diary.

Checklist for clearing down a function suite

All glassware removed from table ☐
All crockery removed from table ☐
All cutlery removed from table ☐
All menus/place cards removed ☐
All ashtrays removed ☐
Table linen removed from table ☐
Soiled linen stored in laundry trolley ☐
Laundry trolley taken to storage area ☐
Glassware to glass wash area/dispense bar ☐
Crockery/cutlery to dishwash area ☐
Waste paper in bins provided ☐
Contents of ashtrays in bins provided ☐
Tables folded and stored correctly ☐
Chairs stacked and stored correctly ☐
Any large items of debris removed ☐
Floor vacuumed ☐
Dance floor swept (if applicable) ☐
Carpet laid back on dance floor (if applicable) ☐
Room layout as per instruction from banqueting manager or head waiter/waitress ☐

Each type of establishment will have a different routine for clearing down and reinstating the service area, but some important points are common to all of them:
- identify next operation
- training of staff
- supervision of staff

- clearing down of service and ancillary areas
- hygiene factors
- safety factors
- security factors such as cash or equipment
- cleaning required
- storage requirements

You should now be aware of the importance of preparing the service areas in relation to the smooth and efficient running of any operation offering food to customers.

Further important reading

Chapter 2 in *Food & Beverage Service* deals with the food and beverage service areas and equipment. Read and study the following sections carefully:

2.2 Stillroom
2.3 Silver room or plate room
2.4 Wash-up
2.5 Hotplate
2.6 Spare linen store

ELEMENT 2c1.1 *Prepare service equipment and areas for table service*

1 Draw up a checklist of all the tasks that are required to be undertaken prior to the opening of the restaurant. This list should be drawn up in the logical order that the tasks should be undertaken.

....

....

....

....

....

....

....

....

....

2 What health and safety legislations should be recognised during the pre-meal operations?

....

....

....

....

....

....

3 What food and hygiene legislations should be recognised during this work?

....

....

....

....

....

....

4 Make a grid showing all the various pieces of equipment in general use within your restaurant. The list should cover all cutlery, crockery, silverware (flatware and hollow ware), as well as any small equipment often associated with stillroom operations (refrigerated units, drink dispensing equipment). Sizes and capacities should be indicated where applicable.

....

....

....

....

....

....

....

5 From your compiled list of crockery state the use/s of each type and size of crockery.

....

....

....

....

....

....

....

6 If your restaurant uses silver, describe the methods that would be employed to ensure the cleanliness of silver. Which items require special attention?

....

....

....

....

....

7 Draw up a rota for a week covering the cleaning of service equipment.

....

....

....

....

....

....

....

....

....

....

8 Draw up a staff rota that recognises the tasks that you have identified in question number 1.

....

....

....

....

....

....

9 What procedures are laid down in your establishment to cover glass breakages and equipment failure?

....

....

....

10 Why is it important to use tinned or packeted tomato juice within two days of opening?

....

....

ELEMENT 2c1.2 *Prepare customers' dining areas for table service*

1 Describe how you would clean the restaurant furniture (this should cover all tables and chairs, lounge furniture, bar stools and chairs, sideboards and metal fittings).

....

....

....

....

....

....

2 What care should be exercised when cleaning table lamps and light fittings?

....

....

3 Draw a plan or diagram of your normal restaurant lay-out. This should show the table numbers as well as the normal number of covers.

4 Draw a diagram of a table for four guests for the following settings: table d'hôte lunch service; à la carte dinner service. You should number and name each item that your restaurant places on the table.

5 The final check normally covers the following: level of heating, ventilation, lighting and music. Why is this the last task and how might it influence the customer?

....

....

....

6   List the types and sizes of linen that you use in the restaurant.

....

....

....

....

7   Describe the procedure for changing restaurant linen.

....

....

....

....

....

....

ELEMENT 2c1.3 *Clear dining and service areas after food service*

1   Draw a post-meal checklist to cover all the normal areas associated with the end of a meal operation. Your list should cover breakfast, lunch and dinner service and include items that are important in recognising health and safety legislation and food hygiene legislation.

....

....

....

....

....

2　What security checks should be built in this list?

　　...

　　...

　　...

3　Recognising food hygiene regulations, what special procedures should be carried
　　out when cleaning down refrigerators, dispensing and small equipment?

　　...

　　...

　　...

4　What is the best way of disposing waste food and rubbish?

　　...

　　...

5　What are the inherent dangers in used ashtrays?

　　...

　　...

Record of Achievement – Completion of Unit 2C1

Candidate's signature　...

Assessor's signature　...

Date　...

PROVIDE A TABLE SERVICE

Duties and responsibilities

One of the restaurant supervisor's main roles will be to allocate duties and responsibilities to each member of staff. Customers may be served in the dining room seven days a week for breakfast, lunch and dinner. The supervisor must determine the number of staff required for each shift to serve the number of guests anticipated. A Staff Duty Rota is usually drawn up for each week. This will detail:

- days worked
- hours of shift
- number of staff per shift
- number of staff on duty each day

An example is given overleaf.

ASSIGNING STATIONS

The area allocated to each food service person is called a station. The number of covers within a station will vary according to staff skills, distance from bar and kitchen area, and number of staff on duty.

In some restaurants, stations are fixed and a member of the restaurant brigade is assigned to this area permanently. In other establishments station allocation may be rotated. In order to cover various busy and quiet periods station size may alter.

The diagrams on page 85 show a restaurant:

- during a quiet time where two sections have been closed off and there are four stations;
- during a busy time with six stations.

BOOKINGS DIARY

Restaurants that accept bookings will keep a Bookings Diary. This will record information about:

- name of customer/host
- telephone number
- number of covers booked
- booking time
- remarks, e.g. dietary requirements, special requests
- signature of person taking the booking

From this information the restaurant supervisor will be able to gauge how busy the service period may be and allocate stations accordingly.

DEPARTMENT: Restaurant   **STAFF DUTY ROTA**   WEEK ENDING: 25 . 9 . 94

	Monday	Tuesday	Wednesday	Thursday	Friday	Saturday	Sunday
Jo	Menus	Linen	Silver	Day off			
Nick		Menus	Linen	Silver	Day off		
Chris			Menus	Linen	Silver	Day off	
Karen				Menus	Linen	Silver	Day off
Mike					Menus	Linen	Silver
Caroline						Menus	Linen
Clint	Linen						Menus
Simon	Silver	Day off					
Liz		Silver	Day off				

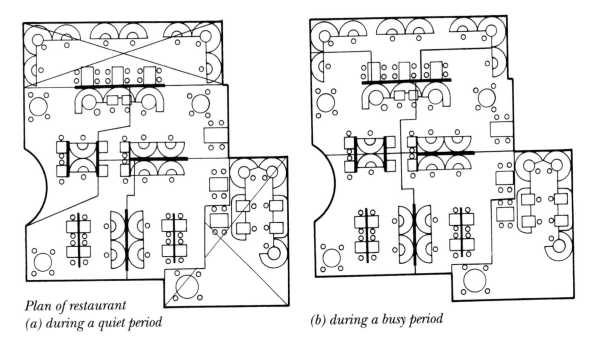

Plan of restaurant
(a) during a quiet period

(b) during a busy period

Table occupancy

To ensure an even workload the restaurant supervisor will allocate bookings to stations. For example, if ten tables are booked for 8.00 pm and there are five stations within the restaurant, each station would be allocated two tables. The supervisor must, of course, take the guests' wishes into account.

In some restaurants, all or most of their customers will be 'chance' guests, i.e. they have arrived without a booking. These customers may be asked to have a drink in the bar until a suitable table is allocated to them.

In most table service restaurants, the supervisor will meet and greet the customers and show them to their table. At this stage the waiter/waitress assigned to that table will take over. First impressions count; therefore, a friendly courteous welcome should reflect a willingness to offer a high standard of service. The degree of formality with which a guest is greeted will depend on the type of establishment.

OFFERING THE MENU

In some establishments the guest may be shown the menu in the bar area before entering the restaurant; in others the menu will be presented when the customer sits at their table.

It is important to draw attention to any special promotions or offers available. Food service staff must be familiar with the composition of all foods on the menu, e.g. the guest may wish to know which dishes would be suitable for a vegetarian or someone on a gluten-free diet. Care must be taken not to mislead customers – do not tell the guest that the grapefruit cocktail is fresh if it is from a tin or that a well cooked sirloin could be ready in just a few minutes.

❖ **Know your menu: remember you are a salesperson so promote the menu.**

TAKING THE ORDER

How the customer's order is taken will depend on establishment procedures. The three main ways are by:
- duplicate check pad
- triplicate check pad
- order keypad

Duplicate check pad

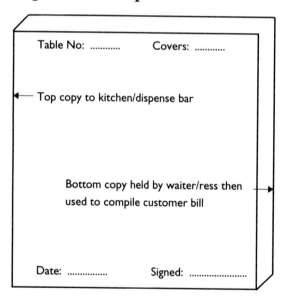

Table No: ....   Covers: ....

⟵ Top copy to kitchen/dispense bar

Bottom copy held by waiter/ress then used to compile customer bill ⟶

Date: ....   Signed: ....

Triplicate check pad

Here the top copy will go to the kitchen/dispense bar; the middle copy (sometimes known as flimsy) to waiting staff and the bottom copy to the cashier to compile the bill.

Completing a check pad

Usually the customer is asked for her/his starter and main course order; the sweet, coffee, etc. would be written on a separate check. Your writing should be neat and legible with any abbreviations easy to understand (see the example opposite).

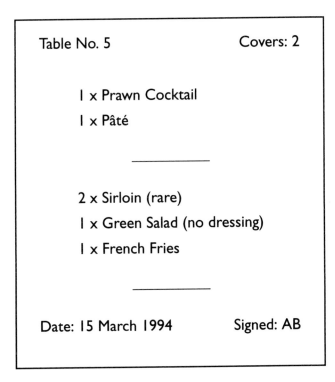

```
┌─────────────────────────────────────────────┐
│                                               │
│   Table No. 5              Covers: 2          │
│                                               │
│                                               │
│      1 x Prawn Cocktail                       │
│      1 x Pâté                                 │
│                                               │
│                                               │
│            ──────────                         │
│                                               │
│                                               │
│      2 x Sirloin (rare)                       │
│      1 x Green Salad (no dressing)            │
│      1 x French Fries                         │
│                                               │
│                                               │
│            ──────────                         │
│                                               │
│                                               │
│   Date: 15 March 1994      Signed: AB         │
│                                               │
└─────────────────────────────────────────────┘
```

Each establishment will have its own methods for taking the customer's order. In some establishments, staff make a note of where the guest is seated in order to remember who is having which dish.

If you are unsure of your customer's order, repeat the order to them for confirmation.

Order key pad

This is a hand-held computer terminal which has a key or code for each menu item. The order is then printed out within the kitchen/dispense bar, etc. This method can save a lot of walking to and from the kitchen hotplate area.

After the customer's order has been taken, the Order of Service should be maintained. This will vary depending on the type of establishment but a framework of serving courses and clearing finished items will emerge. This is discussed in Unit 2C5 Provide a Silver Service.

ELEMENT 2C2.1 *Greet customers and take orders*

1 Draw up a chart, either a bar graph or a pie chart, which illustrates the variety of customers who use your establishments. The chart should show the number of customers such as children, those with mobility difficulties or hearing impairment,

those who have and who have not made a booking, and large parties.

2 Does your establishment have a procedure in dealing with the following types of clients: young children; persons with a mobility difficulty? State your company's policy.

....

....

....

....

3 On occasions a small party of 14 or more may decide to use your establishment without booking in advance. How would you deal with the organiser who wishes the party to be seated at one table?

....

....

....

....

4 How often are you requested to serve certain dietary foods? Can you categorise this special need under particular headings? Discount any vegetarian or vegan dishes.

....

....

....

....

5 Categorise vegetarian and vegan requirements from your own menu.

....

....

....

....

6 If a customer asked for a 'gluten-free' product, what could you offer?

....

....

....

....

7 Provide a sample of your Restaurant Bookings Diary covering a normal mid-week operation and from a very busy lunch/dinner operation. From these sheets, is it possible to ascertain a method which is used in allocating tables to stations in the restaurant?

....

....

....

....

8 Why is it so important to work to some logic in scheduling the table occupancy? What is liable to happen if the first eight parties were put onto the one station?

....

....

....

9 How would you avoid contravening any Trades Description Legislation?

....

....

....

10 Offer an accurate waiter's food-check for a party of six persons who decide to dine from the 'à la carte'. They will have different starters, three main courses, a nominated selection of vegetables, potatoes and green salads. This will be followed by sweets and biscuits and cheese, finishing with coffee. The check should be correctly priced. Should the total price for the party be included?

....

....

....

....

....

....

11 Describe the ten most popular dishes in your restaurant. Imagine that you are describing these dishes to overseas visitors.

....

....

....

....

....

....

....

....

....

....

....

....

ELEMENT 2C2.2 *Serve customers' orders*

1 List the items on your menus that are normally served on **plates** and those normally only served on **silvers**.

....

....

....

....

2 List the types of trolleys that are in popular usage in most restaurants.

....

....

....

....

3   List the dishes that are normally served from a trolley in your restaurant.

   ....

   ....

   ....

   ....

4   List the proprietary sauces and accompaniments that your establishment uses.

   ....

   ....

   ....

   ....

5   Given the choice would you change this list and what would you change it to?

   ....

   ....

   ....

6   Draw a diagram of a plated meal consisting of: chicken sauté, parisienne potatoes, mange tout and mixed green salad.

7   From the laid down procedure of your establishment, how do you ascertain that the correct dish has been served, in the correct manner, correct amount, and the quality of food is most acceptable to the customer?

....

....

....

....

....

....

ELEMENT 2c2.3   *Maintain dining and service areas*

1   List the napkin folds that you use in your restaurant.

....

....

....

....

2   What folds do you use for special parties, small functions, formal dinner parties?

....

....

....

....

3 When is it most appropriate to use slipcloths?

....

....

....

....

4 What 'security and safety checks' should be carried out periodically during meal times and particularly at the end of service?

....

....

....

....

5 Draw up a post-meal check list that operates in your establishment.

....

....

....

....

....

6 What procedures are laid down to deal with paper refuse, food wastage and broken glassware?

....

....

....

....

....

7   Using the normal place setting in your establishment, list the replacement cost of each item (this should cover crockery, glassware and cutlery).

....

....

....

....

....

....

....

....

Record of Achievement – Completion of Unit 2C2

Candidate's signature   ....

Assessor's signature   ....

Date   ....

Unit 2C3

PROVIDE A TABLE DRINK SERVICE

Preparation of bar area

Prior to a bar opening, several duties must be carried out: this is part of the mise-en-place. The bar itself will often be the focal point of the room in which it is situated. It is important that it always looks clean and tidy. The appearance of the bar can often be improved by putting an attractive display on or behind it.

Bottles should always be wiped and labels must always face forwards towards the customer. When stocks are replenished the bottles left on the shelves must be brought forward and the new stocks added at the back. This is also a good time to give the shelves a thorough clean. Empty bottles, bottle tops, etc. must be sorted out and removed from the bar. Ideally this should be completed at the end of service; failing this it is essential to ensure that all 'empties' are removed prior to opening time.

The type of bar sundries required will depend on the style of service being offered: generally the more up-market the service the greater the number of sundries. These may include:

- dishes of nuts, gherkins, crisps, etc., which are laid out and replenished during service;
- cocktail cherries and olives for martinis and other mixed drinks;
- cocktail sticks, bitters (e.g. angostura);
- cocktail shakers, blenders, mixers, strainers, spoons, etc.;
- ice crusher;
- ice, bucket and tongs;
- soda syphon;
- price lists;
- orange and lemon twists;
- orange and lemon slices;
- coasters and drip mats.

Individual bars will have their own policies and procedures regarding the layout of the bar area. To ensure a smooth service the layout of sundry items should be carefully considered. Once a system has been adopted staff become accustomed to operating in a particular way.

Service of spirits

MEASURES

Spirits are usually served by measure. This can vary from ¼ gill (more commonly ⅕ gill in Scotland) to ⅙ gill in England. By law the restaurant or bar must display a notice stating the measure in which gin, vodka, whisky and rum are sold. This will change to metric measures (ml) after 31 December 1994.

The customer may order a single (one measure) or a 'large one' or double (two measures). Often the customer will ask for a certain brand of spirit which should be served if in stock. If it is not available, the customer should be informed and an alternative brand offered. The spirit can be measured by optic or jigger measure.

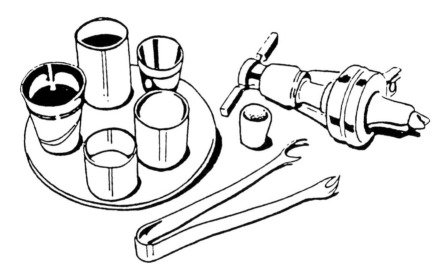

OPTICS

Optics are measuring units made of glass and metal fitted with a release valve which is fitted on top of bottles of spirits, vermouths, etc. The bottles are then inverted and supported in an upside-down position. An accurate measure of liquor is dispensed when a glass is pushed up firmly towards the release valve.

Optics are usually used for the best-selling brands of drink as they are quick and efficient to use. Cocktail or up-market bars may decide against the use of optic measures due to the 'quantity not quality' image they may hold for some customers.

JIGGERS

Jigger measures are used when an optic is not in position. This is often the case for drinks that do not have such a high turnover. Jiggers come in two sizes. The smaller measure, usually ⅕ gill, is used for a single portion of spirit, while the larger one, ⅖ gill, is used for either a double measure of spirit or a single measure of fortified wine, e.g.

port, sherry and vermouth.

   Jigger measures must be rinsed out after each use and placed upside down on the jigger drainer.

GLASSES

The type of glass used to serve spirits in will depend on the establishment. Here are pictures of some of the more common ones.

Wine, mixers, juice and spirit glasses

Beer

Cocktail

Champagne/Sparkling wine

Sherry/Liqueurs

WITH OR WITHOUT MIXERS

Some spirits, e.g. malt whisky and brandy, are enjoyed without the addition of any mixer. Brandy should be served in a brandy goblet so the customer may savour the bouquet. Malt whisky and brandy should never be served with ice unless the customer requires it.

Spirits with a less powerful aroma and taste are often made into long drinks with the addition of a mixer. The most usual of these include:

- for whisky: soda water, ginger ale or plain water
- for gin: tonic water, bitter lemon or ginger ale
- for brandy: soda water or ginger ale
- for vodka: fresh orange, tonic water, lime cordial or cola
- for rum: cola or peppermint cordial

Correct handling and cleaning of glassware

HANDLING

Correct handling of glassware is very important both during table service and bar counter service. If the establishment is operating table service, there should be a drinks mat for each glass.

It should always be remembered that while working behind a bar most bar staff are in full view of the customer. This makes hygiene extremely important. Glasses, bottles, measures, etc. and all work surfaces must be kept clean at all times. In a very busy bar this can become a problem but keeping the work area tidy leads to greater efficiency and speed of service in the long run.

Let's see what you know about this. How should a bar person handle clean or dirty glasses and how should glasses be carried for silver service or preparation? Turn to the pictures on the next page to check your answers.

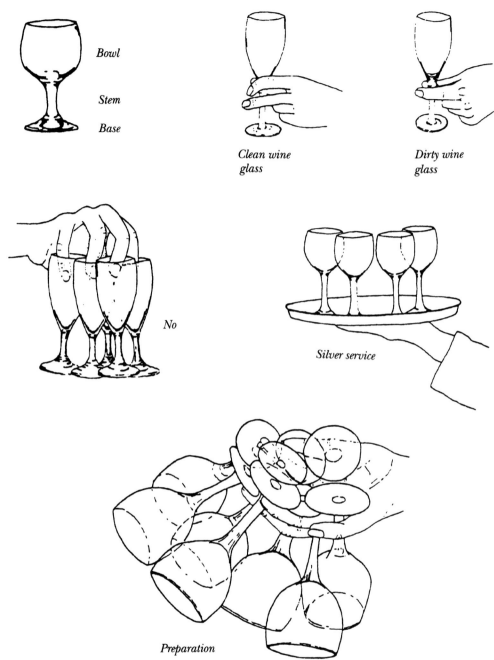

Bowl

Stem

Base

Clean wine
glass

Dirty wine
glass

No

Silver service

Preparation

Handling of glassware

CLEANING

Glasses used for bar service should be stored and cleaned according to the advice in
Unit G2 on page 22.

Service of beer and cider

Beers and cider are usually either draught or bottled.

BOTTLED BEERS AND CIDER

Bottled beer and cider should be kept at a constant cool temperature on a cooling shelf. These are manufactured to hold between 20 and 120 bottles of lager, beer, cider, fruit juices and minerals depending on the bar's turnover of such drinks.

DRAUGHT BEERS AND CIDER

Draught beer may pass through an in-line cooler which lowers the temperature of the beer as it flows through. The cooler is located between the cask or keg and the service pump. In-line coolers are especially important when the bar has no cool underground cellar or when the kegs and casks being used are stored behind the bar counter.

Take care when using pressurised kegs and CO_2 cylinders which are used to make keg beer 'lively', e.g. give it a head. Always follow the operating instructions for the unit.

When pouring draught beer, always tilt the glass and allow the beer to run down the side of the glass. If the machinery is properly maintained, a head of approximately 2 cm should form on the top of the beer as the glass is slowly tilted to a vertical position. Draught cider does not form a 'head', but it should always be 'starbright' and have a clean smell. Draught beer and cider are usually sold by the pint or half pint.

OPENING BOTTLED BEER AND CIDER

Beer and cider bottle tops are removed with a crown cork opener. These are generally attached to the bar top and have a plastic tray which catches the tops as they fall. These trays should be emptied and washed out at the end of every service or at regular intervals throughout the service.

SERVING BOTTLED BEER

Wherever possible, bar staff should face the customer while pouring drinks. When pouring a bottle of beer, the label should be towards the customer. The bottle should be held at an angle of 45° in one hand and the glass at a similar angle in the other. Bottled beer should be poured gently at first with the bottle raised slightly higher as the glass gets fuller. This gives the beer a head and makes for a more presentable drink.

To serve lager and lime, always pour the lager first then add the lime. To serve a shandy, always put the lemonade into the glass first.

Bottled beer should never be shaken-up as this will cause the beer to spray everywhere when opened. Bottled beer is usually served from a ½ pt (10 oz, 3 dl) bottle and poured into a 12 oz (¾ dl) glass. The type of glass used will depend on the establishment and the type of beer, e.g. lager, stout, bitter, etc. being poured.

Legislation

RESTAURANT LICENCE

In order to qualify for such a licence the premises must be intended to be used for the provision of a main meal at midday or in the evening, or both. The licence prohibits the sale or supply of intoxicating liquor, except for consumption at a table meal (this meal need not necessarily be a customary main meal).

RESIDENTIAL LICENCE

In order to qualify for this type of licence the premises must be used or intended to be used for board and lodgings, including breakfast and at least one of the customary main meals.

The conditions of the licence prohibits the sale or supply of intoxicating liquor, except to residents or their private friends who are entertained at their own expense, for consumption either on the premises or with a meal supplied but to be eaten off the premises.

A residential licence should provide a 'dry room' condition. This is providing paying guests with a room with sitting accommodation, which is not used for sleeping, service of food or consumption of intoxicating liquor.

A licence may, however, be granted without the above conditions, if there is a special reason for not imposing the requirement. If there is a change in circumstances then the conditions may be added on at a later date.

COMBINED RESIDENTIAL AND RESTAURANT LICENCE

This licence combines the requirements of both of the above licences. In addition non-alcoholic drinks, including water, must be available at all meals served in the premises. Let's look at the law in more detail.

WEIGHTS AND MEASURES

A notice must be displayed, which gives a clear indication of the measures used for the sale of whisky, vodka, gin and rum. The measures can be ¼, ⅕ or ⅙ of a gill. Remember a gill is a ¼ pint. Mixed drinks of three or more drinks are exempt from this law. Draught beer and cider may be sold by ⅓, ½ or multiples of ½ pints.

MEASURES

If wine is sold in carafes or by the glass, then a notice must be displayed prominently showing how much wine per unit is served.

YOUNG PERSONS

Children under the age of 14 years must not be allowed in any bar. Remember this does not mean children of the licensee or a child in residence.

A child may pass through a bar if there is no other way to reach another part of the premises. Young persons aged 14 to 16 years may be allowed into a bar with an adult but may not buy or consume alcohol. A licensee and his/her staff must not knowingly allow any person under the age of 18 to purchase or consume alcohol in a bar or licensed premises.

DRINKS

Remember it is an offence to permit drunkenness or rowdy behaviour on the premises.

PERMITTED HOURS

Liquor must not be sold out of permitted hours. Extensions to permitted hours may be applied for. A resident may entertain an unlimited number of friends to drink so long as it is the resident who pays.

LICENSEE'S RESPONSIBILITY

The licensee should aim to provide a pleasant environment for the clientele. A list should be displayed outlining the laws that have been produced to protect the public. The licensee must at all times adhere to the law.

ELEMENT 2C3.1 *Provide a table drink service*

1 Write down what you think the glasses shown here would be used for.

2 Promoting and selling a variety of beverages is very much part of your everyday activities. What promotional leaflets, tent-cards, posters or special features does your establishment employ to help sell these beverages?

....

....

....

....

....

3 Supply a check list that applies to your beverages service operations, covering pre-meal, meal, and post-meal activities.

....

....

....

....

....

....

4 Compile a complete list of all equipment that is used for the service of alcoholic and non-alcoholic beverages within your establishment. (This should be divided into glassware, trays, silverware, service linen and small equipment.)

....

....

....

....

....

....

5 List the notices that should be on display in a licensed restaurant. Give reasons for the display of each notice, and where each notice is displayed.

....

....

....

....

6 From your knowledge of the Hygiene Regulations, state those that are directly related to licensed premises.

....

....

....

....

7 What type of license does your establishment operate under?

....

8 Draw a grid from your restaurant bar tariff and wine list that shows the price, ingredients, relative strength and possible alternative beverages that are on offer within your restaurant.

9 What measure is used for the dispensing of spirits? What spirits must always be dispensed in single or multiples of this measure?

....

10 What procedures does your establishment take when dealing with a person who is behaving in a disorderly, drunken or violent manner?

....

....

11 Are there any warning signs that might help to overcome this situation?

....

....

12 State the licensing laws as they affect young persons in your restaurant.

....

....

....

....

Record of Achievement – Completion of Unit 2C3

Candidate's signature ....

Assessor's signature ....

Date ....

Unit 2C4

PROVIDE A CARVERY OR BUFFET SERVICE

Assisted service

This type of service combines table and self service. The two most popular forms are carvery-style operations and buffets.

CARVERY-STYLE OPERATIONS

An example of a carvery menu could be:

Creamy Chicken Liver Pâté
Chilled Melon Cocktail
Avocado with Prawn Marie Rose
Minestroni Soup

Roast Prime Rib of Beef served with Yorkshire Pudding and Horseradish Sauce
Roast Loin of Pork with Sage and Onion Stuffing and Apple Sauce
Roast Leg of Lamb with Mint Jelly
Cold Honey Roast Ham

Boiled Potatoes
Roast Potatoes
Buttered Carrots
Green Beans
Selection of Salads

Double Chocolate Chip Ice-Cream
Strawberry Gâteau
Chocolate Cheesecake
Fresh Fruit Salad
Selection of Scottish Cheeses

Coffee and Mints

Carvery-style operations are found within large hotels, public houses and speciality restaurants, e.g. Toby Grill, a nationwide chain of carvery-type restaurants. The menu usually comprises of a three course set menu for a fixed price with a selection of four or five starters, three to four roast meats and a choice of cold sweets and ice-creams (see below). Guests are usually served their starter, sweet and coffee by a food service person, but go to the carvery to be served their main course. The person behind the carvery is usually in chef's whites. She/he will assist the guest by carving a suitable portion of meat.

There are two main advantages in offering a carvery-type menu:

- The visual impact of the carvery increases sales.
- The perception of 'value for money' is increased as the customer decides on portion size.

BUFFETS

Buffets involve the presentation of a wide selection of food items on a buffet table or purpose-built counter from which customers help themselves or are assisted by a member of staff serving from behind the buffet. This style of service is often used for functions. The service of breakfast is often now carried out from a buffet within the dining room.

The main advantage to the caterer is that less waiting staff are required. In order that a large number of people may be served over a fairly short period of time, several service points may offer the same menu. This avoids long queues. An ideal buffet layout is shown opposite.

- The buffet must be within easy reach of the kitchen, stillroom and wash-up.
- There must be space to allow guests to move freely from their seat to the buffet and back.
- There must be space for staff to serve behind the buffet.

Setting up the buffet/carvery area

The staff duties may be divided into the following areas: cold display area; hot display area; dining area. In order to ensure that all duties are carried out, checklists may be used.

PRE-SERVICE

Cold display area

- Clean display cabinet and counter area.
- Check that cold display is switched on: record temperature.
- Familiarise yourself with cold items on menu:
  - translation and composition
  - presentation
  - portioning
  - display
  - service
- Plan display of food items as per company procedures.
- Collect food items from kitchen.
- Count out and polish all crockery required for service.

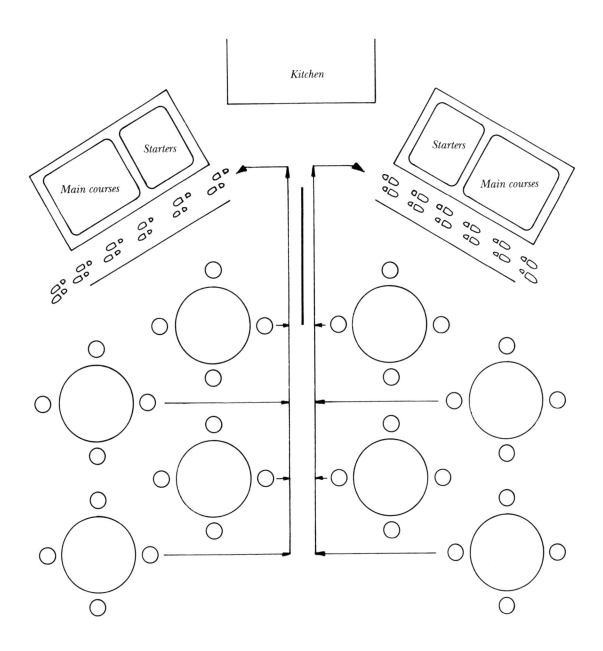

Buffet layout

- Display food attractively.
- Display accompaniments.
- Collect service equipment.
- Equipment check.
- Uniform check.

Hot display area
- Clean counter area.
- Switch on hot plate or serving equipment.
- Count out and polish all crockery required for service.
- Familiarise yourself with hot items on the menu:
    translation and composition
    presentation
    portioning
    display
    service
- Plan layout of food on display area.
- Lay out necessary serving equipment.
- Display accompaniments.
- Collect food from kitchen.
- Display food attractively, check positioning is correct.
- Check equipment and service clothes available.
- Uniform check.

Dining area
The preparation required for the dining area will depend on the type of meal being served and on company policy. The dining area will be prepared and set up in the same method as table service. This will include cleaning the restaurant area, stocking side stations, laying tables and other mise-en-place duties.

The cutlery that is laid on the table will depend on the menu items and service style. For a carvery operation the cover may be a joint knife and fork, side plate and side knife. Cutlery for starters and sweets would be brought with the items being served.

DURING SERVICE

It is important that the buffet or carvery area looks attractive throughout the service period. The last guest should have just as good an impression of standards of layout and presentation as the first. This can only be achieved by constant attention to detail.
- Keep display areas clean at all times.
- Rearrange display as items are taken by customers.
- Replenish dishes as required.
- Serve meals at correct temperature.
- Ensure portion control procedures are maintained.
- Replenish accompaniments as required.

- Be pleasant and attentive to customers needs.

The dining area, tables, sideboard, etc. must also be kept clean and tidy throughout the service period. Waste food, dirties, etc. should be removed to the dishwash area without delay.

POST-SERVICE

In order to maintain a high standard staff must be trained to ensure that all duties have been carried out.

Cold display area
- Remove cold items to the larder.
- Remove service cutlery to wash-up.
- Turn off cold display cabinet.
- Clean display area.

Hot display area
- Switch off hot display.
- Remove left-over food and return it to kitchen.
- Remove service cutlery to wash-up.
- Clean hot display area.
- Remove all clean crockery to storage area.
- Clean any shelves, lamps, etc.

Dining area
- All dirty crockery trays, etc. to wash-up.
- All refuse to wash-up.
- Clear linen from tables or wipe table tops or mats.
- Rearrange furniture if required.
- Return cruets, ashtrays, butter dishes, etc. to storage area.
- Set up dining area as per instructions.

Special function buffets

A form of buffet service is often used for special functions. These may be classed into three categories:
- Knife and fork: This is where the guests are seated at a table that will be fully laid up for the number of courses to be consumed.
- Fork buffet: This is where the guest may be standing whilst eating only with a fork small items of food off a plate. Some chairs may be provided for elderly guests.
- Finger buffet: In this situation no cutlery is required as all the food may be eaten without cutlery, e.g. sandwiches, small vol-au-vents, individual quiches, pizza slices, sausage rolls, etc.

A customer wishing to organise a buffet for a function will usually be shown several menu choices each offering different menu items at differing prices. For example:

Buffet (knife and fork) – Number:
Fresh Tomato Soup
Smoked Trout Mousse
Melon with Parma Ham

Duck Casserole with Cherries
Cold Smoked Chicken Breast
Fillet of Sole with Lemon

Assorted Salads and Potatoes

Toffee Caramel Choux Pastries
Coffee and Mints

Buffet (fork) – Number:
Beef Stroganoff with Rice
Gougons of Sole
Chicken Fillets in a Herb Sauce

Assorted Salads

Coffee Eclairs
Chocolate Baskets

BREAKFAST BUFFET

As we have already discussed many hotels have replaced traditional breakfast service with a breakfast buffet: this cuts down on the number of staff required both in the dining room and kitchen whilst increasing sales due to the visual impact of the buffet.

In most cases guests will be served with hot beverages and fresh toast by a food service person but will be helped at the buffet to any other menu item they require. This gives the guest a greater choice as they can see the food before making their selection.

LAYING UP A BUFFET

The food on the buffet table must look appealing to the guests. This can be achieved by a careful mixing of colours, textures and presentation techniques. More expensive menu items may be placed in less accessible areas; some buffets may feature displays such as an ice or fat carving as a focus of attention. Foods may be placed at different heights to give interest and a feeling of plenty. Sauces and accompaniments should be placed next to the items they are to accompany.

SERVING FROM A BUFFET COUNTER

Establishment procedures will dictate whether the guest is served or allowed to help themselves. In order to maintain portion control and speed up service a member of staff will usually serve at least part of the meal, e.g. the more expensive foods such as meats, poultry, salmon, etc.

In order to avoid a lot of waste customers should be encouraged not to load up their plates but to return if they require more. It is important to remember safety and hygiene points: take care with hot plates, serving dishes, etc. and never allow food to stand uncovered in a warm room for too long or bacteria will rapidly multiply. Hot food should be covered as often as possible to retain the heat. Some establishments may use temperature probes to ensure food is not in the danger zones (5–63°C) for any length of time.

ELEMENT 2C4.1 *Prepare and maintain a carvery or buffet display*

1 List the points that should be remembered when dealing with customers in a polite and helpful manner.

....

....

....

....

2 From your knowledge of 'in-house' procedures, how would you assist the following types of customers?

a) Young children ....

....

....

b) Wheelchair customers ....

....

....

c) Elderly customers ....

....

....

d) Customers with walking difficulties or sight impairment ....

....

....

3 Draw up a staffing schedule which insures all the necessary and appropriate work is carried out in the preparation of a carvery or buffet layout.

4 List the types of carvery/buffet 'set-ups' that are used in your establishment. These may include: breakfast service; lunch or dinner service; wedding breakfasts; afternoon tea service.

....

....

....

....

....

....

5 Draw a diagram of the carvery/buffet to cover each of the types your establishment uses. You should note the following and show on the diagram:
- numbers expected for service
- area of food display
- types of food being offered
- position of large equipment and small utensils
- position of any display feature
- supply sample buffet/carvery menus.

6 Draw up a hygiene list to cover all large equipment and small utensils that you use.

....

....

....

....

....

7 Draw up a checklist that helps to monitor the temperature control of food on display (hot and cold).

....

....

....

....

....

....

....

....

....

....

8 The display of food and their accompaniments are an important feature and selling point of all buffet and carvery presentations. List the points that are important along with reasons which show this importance to selling.

....

....

....

....

....

....

9 Portion control must be exercised when food is offered to customers, otherwise profitability will suffer. Suggest how 'portion control' may be achieved.

....

....

....

....

10 What 'in-house' procedures should be adopted when it comes to replenishing dishes? Why is this so important, particularly half way through a buffet or carvery service?

....

....

....

....

....

....

11 List the safety points that staff should be aware of.

....

....

....

....

....

....

ELEMENT 2C4.2 *Serve customers at the carvery or buffet*

1 List the menu items as identified in 2C4.1 questions 4 and 5 and give the main selling feature of each item. This may be drawn up in a grid format as detailed:

Menu Item	Buffet/Carvery Type*					Selling Points
	A	B	C	D	E	

*List types currently used in your establishment.

2 List the 'in-house' procedures that deal with the following:

• Greeting customers ....

    ....

• Food displays ....

    ....

• Portion control ....

    ....

• Plate and dish displays ....

    ....

- Health and safety including hygiene requirements ....

....

ELEMENT 2C4.3 *Maintain customer dining areas*

1 How would you deal with food/sauce spillages on the buffet/carvery table or floor area?

....

....

....

2 How would you replace or correctly deal with linen that has unsightly food spillage marks?

....

....

....

3 How would you deal with tables that require to be cleaned (as in 2 above) or reset for the 'next sitting'?

....

....

....

4 List the reasons for ensuring that not only the buffet/carvery but also the customer areas are kept clean and tidy.

....

....

....

Record of Achievement – Completion of Unit 2C4

Candidate's signature   ....

Assessor's signature   ....

Date   ....

PROVIDE A SILVER SERVICE

On the following pages we will examine the technical skills required for silver service. It is important to note that you will be assessed on your ability to carry these out proficiently.

During the table service of lunch and dinner a framework emerges; it varies from establishment to establishment in small respects but the example below is a general guideline. It is usually referred to as the 'Order of Service'.

Order of service

The following procedures should be adopted during the service of lunch or dinner. The headwaiter/waitress should seat guests holding out chairs for them. He/she should then unfold the napkin and place it over the guest's lap, then present the menu.

- The server should greet the guests as soon as possible after they are seated. The wine waiter may enquire if they wish to order aperitifs before their meal. Rolls and Melba Toast should be offered and butter placed on the table.
- Menus should be presented to host and guests.
- Before the order is taken, the guests should be advised of items, such as appetisers, not shown on the menu. It is essential that the server has up-to-date knowledge of the menu, so that she/he is able to translate culinary items and basic preparation of all items.
- When taking the order, the server should have eye contact with each guest as the order is given and question any request or enquiry not fully understood.
- When the dinner order is complete, remove the menu from the table. Offer the wine list if it has not already been requested.
- If wine is ordered, it should be brought to the table and presented to the host. The server should then enquire as to when the wine is to be poured. Follow the procedure of service as described by the house.
- Take meal order to kitchen and relay any special requests to the Chef at this time.
- Change covers where required. Serve hors d'oeuvres.
- From this point on, the routine service of removing soiled bar glasses, replenishing rolls, butter and clean ashtrays should be performed after a course is cleared and before the next course is served. Such consideration allows the guests to enjoy each course without service interruptions. The food servers should pay particular attention to the clearing of soiled dishes and ensure that all guests at the table have finished their course before any clearing begins.

- Remove hors d'oeuvre plates and soiled flatware
- Serve soup course.
- Remove soup plates and under-plates.
- If the wine has been ordered to be served with the main course, proceed with wine service at this time.
- Collect the main course from the kitchen. Be sure that any special requests have been fulfilled by the Chef.
- Serve main course. Offer a word of caution to guests if serving plates are hot. Serve appropriate accompaniments.
- Allow a minute or two before asking guests if everything is in order. A negative response should be attended to immediately. An apology should be made to the guest and the plate removed to the kitchen for correction by the Chef. Wait in the kitchen until the food is ready to be returned to the table.
- Top up wine glasses during the main course.
- Remove main course dishes and flatware.
- Remove side plates, butter dish, melba toast and cruet from the table. Table top should be crumbed down. If wine service is completed, empty glasses and bottles should be removed from the table at this time.
- Inform guests of dessert items that are available for the day and take order for desserts and beverages.
- Serve dessert course.
- Remove dessert dishes.
- Serve coffee.
- Server should ask if after dinner drinks are desired.
- Serve after dinner drinks if required.
- Refill coffee cups.
- Present bill upon request. Return any cash change to the host on a side plate or small salver.
- Server should thank guests for their kindness as they leave.
- Check table tops, chairs and floor area for forgotten articles.
- Clear table and reset if needed.

As well as an Order of Service there are several points of service that are adhered to. Read these carefully and try to remember them always; after a while they will become second nature.

❖ Points of Service

1 Always place clean plates from Right.
2 Always serve food from Left.
3 Always remove dirty plates from Right.
4 Always serve coffee and all liquids (beverages) from Right.
5 Always serve plated food from Left.

6   Always serve salad crescents from Left.
7   Remember above points only if convenient to the customer.

Taking the guests' order

It is important to remember your role as a salesperson. Suggest to the guests items on the menu, thus focusing attention on dishes you may have been asked to promote. Use visual aids, e.g. refer to the carving trolley, draw attention to special promotional offers. It is essential to have a good knowledge of the menu. Guests may wish to enquire about ingredients due to food allergies or taste.

   Whilst giving suggestions and taking the order, stand to the left of the host. Try to estimate what kind of group the guests are, e.g. age, nature of party, etc. This may help with recommending certain dishes. Take orders through the host and advise if a dish will take longer than average time to prepare. (This is especially important if children are present.)

Serving the guests

❖ **Remember**
1   The host is served last except during banquets.
2   The lady on the host's right should be served first, then all the other ladies, then gentlemen.
3   In an all female party, serve the eldest lady first.
4   Do not assume the host will always be a man.

CARRYING THREE PLATES

When carrying plates:
•   Keep the plates level.
•   Keep fingers away from plated food.
•   Practice will build up strength in your wrists.

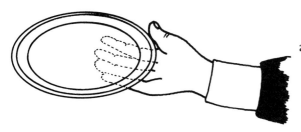

a) Pick up first plate in right hand.

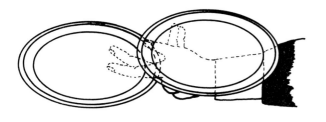

b) Transfer plate to left hand.

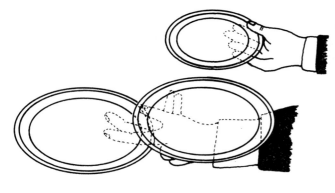

c) Transfer second plate to left hand and pick up third plate.

HOLDING A SERVICE SPOON AND FORK

In order to serve food from a flat silver or dish onto the guest plate, a spoon and fork are used. This technique can be mastered by most people within a short space of time.

a) Hold spoon and fork together, with the service fork on top of the service spoon.

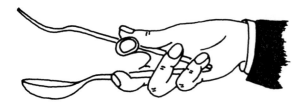

b) Hold service spoon in position; use forefinger and thumb to hold the handle of the service fork.

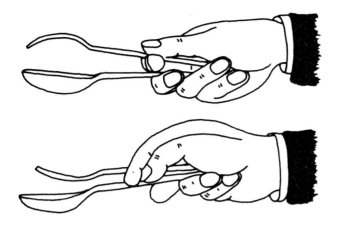

c) Turn fork over to serve rounded items, e.g. bread rolls.

d) This position may be used to serve fish fillets, omelettes, etc.

SPECIALIST EQUIPMENT AND ITS USE

Equipment	*Dish*
Asparagus holder	For holding asparagus spears when eating
Pastry slice	For serving portions of gateau on sweet trolley
Oyster fork	Shellfish cocktail/oysters
Pastry fork	Afternoon tea
Corn-on-the-cob holders	Corn-on-the-cob (one to pierce each end)
Lobster pick	Lobster (to extract the flesh from the claw)
Butter knife	Butter dish
Caviar knife	Has a short broad blade for spreading the caviar.
Fruit knife and fork	Dessert: fruit basket
Nutcrackers	Dessert: fruit basket
Grape scissors	For cutting and holding a portion of grapes
Grapefruit spoon	Grapefruit halves
Ice-cream spoon	For all ice-cream dishes served in coupes
Sundae spoon	Ice-cream sweet in a tall glass
Snail tongs	For holding the snail shell
Snail dish	Round with two ears, having six indentations to hold one portion (6) of snails
Snail fork	For extracting the snail from shell
Cheese knife	Cheese board
Stilton scoop	Service of stilton cheese
Silver skewers	Kebabs: used for attractive presentation
Preserve spoon	For jam dish
Mustard spoon	For mustard pot
Sugar tongs	For cube sugar

SERVING FROM A SILVER

Most main course dishes are silver served from a silver (or 'flat') onto the customers' empty plates. Place empty plate in front of customer from right-hand side.

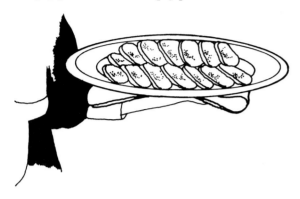

a) Hold silver flat on the left hand and arm; use a service cloth for protection.

b) Serve from the left-hand side of the customer.

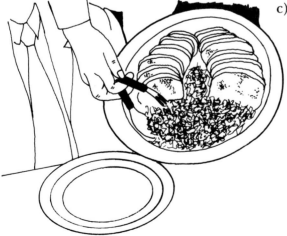

c) Hold silver as near to the customer's plate as possible.

SERVING FROM A DEEP DISH

Vegetables and potatoes are usually served from deep vegetable dishes. These are put on a liner to allow the service of several types at once. To avoid food becoming mixed together a separate set of service cutlery is required for each item.

Care should be taken with appearance and portion control.

SERVING ACCOMPANIMENTS

These are served to complement and enhance the flavour of foods.

Sauces are usually served to the guest from a sauce boat on a liner with a sauce ladle. Some very thin sauces may be poured. Sauce is served from the left of the customer with due regard to presentation appearance and portion control.

a) Hold the sauceboat and liner on the left hand.

b) Position the sauceboat close to the
   guest plate. Enquire if guest wishes
   sauce.

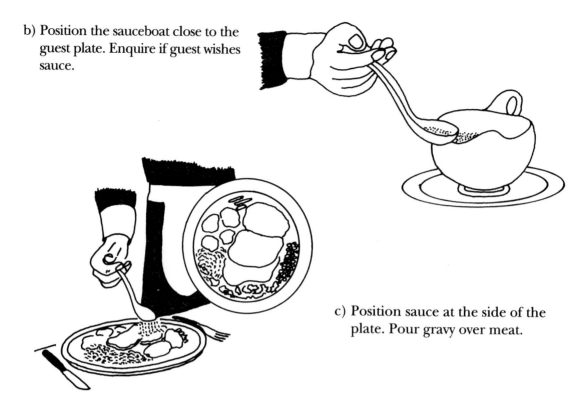

c) Position sauce at the side of the
   plate. Pour gravy over meat.

Here is a list of some of the dishes you may serve with their accompaniments.

Dish	*Accompaniment*
Hors d'oeuvre	Olive oil and vinegar
Prawn cocktail	Brown bread and butter, cayenne pepper, pepper mill
Smoked salmon	Brown bread and butter, cayenne pepper, pepper mill
Melon	Castor sugar and ground ginger
Pâté maison	Hot toast
Minestrone	Grated parmesan cheese
Clear turtle soup	Cheese straws
Cold poached salmon	Mayonnaise
Deep fried breadcrumbed fish	Tartare sauce
Roast leg of lamb	Mint sauce or redcurrant jelly, gravy
Roast leg of mutton	Redcurrant jelly or mint sauce, gravy
Roast pork	Apple sauce, gravy, English mustard
Grilled steaks	English and French mustard
Roast turkey	Cranberry sauce
Cheese and biscuits	Celery, radishes, spring onions, etc.
Coffee	Petit fours, after-dinner mints

CLEARING PLATES

Clear from the right hand side. Step back from each customer. Work quickly and quietly. Never carry too many plates.

a) First dirty joint plate cleared.

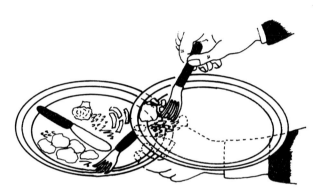

b) Second dirty joint plate cleared.
Note position of forks and knives.

CLEARING OTHER EQUIPMENT

To leave the table as clear and tidy as possible throughout the service of a meal, it is important to remove any items no longer required. A service plate is used to remove items from a table, e.g. unused covers, cruets, butter, dishes, ashtrays, etc.

After the main course has been served, any unused cutlery should be cleared using a service plate. After the main course is finished and plates and cutlery have been cleared, butter dishes and cruets should be removed.

Coupes and liners may be cleared using a small salver which should be held on one hand and arm, never layed down on the table.

CRUMBING DOWN

After the clearing process has been carried out, breadcrumbs and other debris may still be found on the table. These are removed by 'crumbing down'. This is achieved by using a service plate with a napkin on it to catch the crumbs, etc. and a waiter's cloth is used to remove crumbs and debris from the table. Any crumbs/debris should be brushed (with the service cloth) from the centre of the place setting onto the service plate.

If a table d'hôte setting is used, the dessert fork is then moved from the head of the place setting to the left-hand side of the cover. The same process takes place on the guest's right-hand side and the dessert spoon is moved down.

This method of crumbing down ensures that all food service staff never, at any time, stretch across the front of a guest.

SERVING CHEESE

Cheese is often served as an alternative to a sweet or as an extra course. It is important for food service staff to name and describe any cheese being offered to the customer.

The cover for cheese, side plate and small knife as well as a butter dish and cruet should be placed on the table before the cheese is served. The cheeseboard is then presented to the guest from the left-hand side.

The customer is served the cheese they wish with due regard to portion control and presentation. A selection of biscuits, e.g. cream crackers, oatcakes and water biscuits, is then offered to the guest. Accompaniments for cheese include celery and radish plus castor sugar for cream cheeses.

SERVING COFFEE

Coffee is usually served to round off the meal. It is important that high standards are maintained during the service of coffee as this will be the guest's final impression of the meal.

Coffee cups should always be warm to prevent the coffee cooling down quickly. Coffee mise-en-place (or 'sets') consisting of demi-tasse, saucer, coffee spoon, coaster and liner may be assembled at the service station and then taken to the table pre-assembled.

Alternatively the mise-en-place may be placed on a salver and assembled in front of the guest. The method chosen would depend on the company policy. It is important that all service staff should adopt the same method.

The method of serving coffee will vary from establishment to establishment. Petit fours are often served with the coffee.

❖ **Remember**

1 The coffee 'sets' are placed in front of the guest.
2 Milk/cream and sugar are placed on the table.
3 A coffee jug or cafetière is placed on the guests' table.
4 Guests help themselves to coffee.
5 Service staff ask if guests require more after a short interval.

Traditional coffee service

- On the palm of your left hand carry a napkin covered salver with coffee pot, milk pot/cream jug and sugar bowl. Make sure coffee and milk are hot.
- Go to the guest's right and ask: 'Do you take your coffee black, sir/madam, or with milk/cream?'
- Ask: 'Do you take sugar?'
- Serve sugar first.

- Rotate the salver to bring coffee pot nearer to the customer's cup.
- Serve the coffee by tilting the pot (see illustration). Fill to about ¼ inch from the brim.
- Serve milk if required in the same way. Pour cream gently so that it floats on the surface of the coffee.
- Move coffee service in towards the guest.
- Return salver to stillroom.

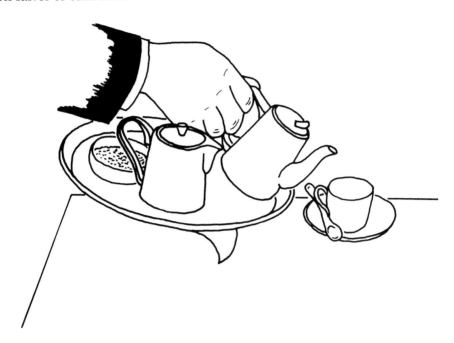

Practical skills checklist

You may find this checklist helpful while building your clearing skills.

Clearing Starter Plates
Dirties cleared from right-hand side of guest. ☐
Clear plates using left hand (clearing hand). ☐
Transfer dirty plate to holding hand (right hand). ☐
First dirty plate held firmly. ☐
Succeeding dirties built on the first. ☐

Clearing Joint Plates
Clear from right-hand side. ☐
Clear using left hand. ☐
Transfer dirty plate to holding hand. ☐
First plate secured. ☐

Joint knife placed under fork. ☐
Debris placed in a triangle formed by handles of joint knife and fork. ☐
Second, third and fourth joint plates cleared. ☐
Debris cleared from upper joint plate onto lower joint plate in each case. ☐

Clearing Side Plates Using Service Salver
Clear from left-hand side. ☐
Thumb of clearing hand placed over knife. ☐
Pass from clearing hand to holding hand. ☐
Succeeding plates built on second plate. ☐
Debris and knives cleared onto silver. ☐

I can:
Hold and manipulate a service spoon and fork. ☐
Carry three plates in a safe manner. ☐
Make correct use of a service salver. ☐
Make correct use of service plate. ☐
Carry clean/dirty glasses in the correct manner. ☐
Carry and use trays. ☐
Clear plates in a professional manner. ☐
Service customer throughout the meal. ☐

So far we have looked in detail at lunch and dinner service within hotels and restaurants offering silver service. It would be impossible to detail every aspect of presentation and service skills for all types of catering. Where the primary method of food service is plate service, a simplified version of the one detailed would be carried out. Cafeteria or counter service would be a simplified version of the plate service, in that the customer collects his/her own plated meal from a counter.

If you have problems, discuss them with your tutor who is there to help.

Important reading

Chapter 5 of *Food and Beverage Service* deals with the food and beverage service sequence. Read and study the following sections carefully:
5.1   Basic technical skills
5.5   The order of service
5.7   Service of food
5.9   Service of non-alcoholic beverages
5.10 Clearing

ELEMENT 2c5.1 *Silver serve food*

1   Complete the following chart

Menu Item	Cover	Accompaniments	Remarks
Smoked Eel			
Snails			
Cantaloup			
Shellfish Cocktail			
Avocado			
Pâté			
Artichoke			

2　What are the five main rules for the service of coffee?

....

....

....

....

....

3　What equipment do you require in the ladling and serving of soup?

....

....

....

4　Draw up an Order of Service that mirrors your workplace.

....

....

....

....

....

....

ELEMENT 2c5.2 *Clear finished courses*

1　Describe the method 'crumbing down'

....

....

....

2 What Health and Safety Legislation must be observed when serving customers?

....

....

....

3 How do you change an ashtray when customers occupy a table?

....

....

....

4 Draw a diagram of how you would load a tray when clearing a table at the end of a meal.

5 How would you deal with a spillage when guests are leaving the table during normal meal times and the table is required for another party of guests who are waiting in the lounge?

....

....

....

....

....

....

Record of Achievement – Completion of Unit 2C5

Candidate's signature ....

Assessor's signature ....

Date ....

PREPARE AND SERVE BOTTLED WINES

In this section we will consider how to serve wines, and also look at the types of service equipment necessary to carry out the service. It is very important that wine is served in the correct way and at the correct temperature. To improve the 'drink experience' it is advisable to use suitable glasses.

Despite a recent trend for bag-in-box wine, the bottle still remains the most popular container for wine.

Wine bottle aspects

Neck: cylinder of even shape for taking the cork

Shoulder: may be square or sloping

Capsule: made of lead foil or plastic, keeps the cork clean

Ullage: amount of space between wine and cork; wine should come half way up the neck

Label: gives information on wine quality, place of origin, contents and strength

Punt: indentation in base adds strength and helps catch sediment in red wine

BOTTLE SHAPE

Each major wine style and region has its characteristic bottle shape and sometimes colour of glass. For example, Bordeaux uses green glass for red wine, clear for white. The 'shoulder' of the bottle helps to impede sediment on its way to the glass decanter. The tall German bottle is almost always green for Moselle and brown for Rhine wine – a reflection of the difference between their sharper and richer flavours.

Bordeaux   *Burgundy*   *Alsace*   *Champagne*

Rhine/Moselle   *Litre bottle*   *Franconia, but also familiar in Portugal*

BOTTLE SIZES

Wine generally comes in three sizes of bottle. Standard (75 cl) is the most popular size. It is possible to get 6–9 glasses from a standard bottle, depending on the size of glass being used. Red wine glasses are usually larger than white wine glasses.

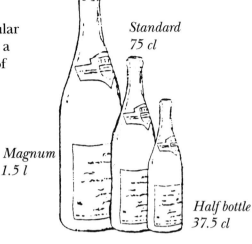

Standard
75 cl

Magnum
1.5 l

Half bottle
37.5 cl

Types of glasses

Jot down below what you think these glasses are used for.

1 ....

2 ....

3 ....

4 ....

5 ....

6 ....

7 ....

8 ....

9 ....

10 ....

Service temperature

It is very important that all wine is served at the correct temperature so that it can be appreciated at its best. Wine should never be cooled quickly such as in the freezer; if it is too cold, it should not be warmed up too quickly, such as in hot water or on top of a heater.

Red wine, once brought to room temperature should not be chilled again, so it is not a good idea to return it to the cellar.

Room temperature is ideal at 17°C. An ideal temperature for a beer cellar is 14°C. Beer and lager should be served cool.

Temperature	Wines
20°C (68°F)	Full-bodied red wines (e.g. Barolo, Medoc, Chateuneuf du Pape)
15°C (59°F)	Lighter red wines (e.g. Beaujolais)
10°C (50°F) (chilled)	Rosé/white wines/champagne (e.g. Anjou rosé, Chablis)
8°C (47°F) (well chilled)	Sweeter white wines (e.g. Sauternes)

Mise en place

Before a wine waiter commences service, he/she must ensure that everything required for the service is to hand. This is called mise en place. It is important for service to be smooth. Equipment may be visible to customers, so keep it tidy and uncluttered.

EQUIPMENT

- Glasses should be clean, free from dust and highly polished. Keep extra glasses ready-to-hand.
- Ashtrays should be clean and ready to use.
- Wine lists should be clean and up-to-date. There should be one for each wine waiter, dispense barman and manager.
- Ice buckets should be kept in the restaurant if there is room, otherwise keep them available nearby. Make sure they are clean. Check the supply of ice.
- Wine decanters should be clean and ready.
- Decanter funnel should be clean and ready.
- Wine baskets should be clean and ready.
- The liqueur and cigar trolley should be stocked, clean and ready. Replenishments for the trolley should be at hand.
- Miscellaneous items such as service trays, straws, matches, iced water, ice, corkscrews, cigar cutter, check pad and pencil, clean napkins, should be available.

Opening a bottle of wine

If this is new to you, you may need to practise quite a lot, although it may not always be possible to practise with the real thing! A good alternative is to purchase corks and a recorking machine (available from any 'home brew' shop). These are not too expensive. You can then fill empty bottles of wine with water and recork them as many times as required. A few grains of sand can act as 'sediment'.

If you do not have one, it is best to purchase a good 'waiter's' corkscrew. This is a good investment!

RIGHT AND WRONG TYPES OF CORKSCREW

Some types of corkscrew are better and easier to use than others. Look carefully at the drawings, then read the descriptions alongside.

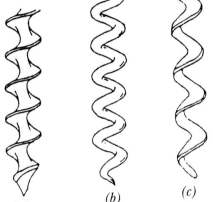

(a) is virtually a gimlet which merely pierces the cork.
(b) is rounded, with a complete spiral to go through the cork, hold it and, without breaking, enable it to be pulled out without damage.
(c) has a sharp edge which will cut into the cork and risk breaking it.

Waiter's corkscrew with penknife (for cutting metal or plastic capsules). It has a lever in the body of the divide plus a prong that incorporates a 'crown' cork remover.

Double screw cork extractor. The top lever inserts the screw, then the lower lever is turned to raise the cork.

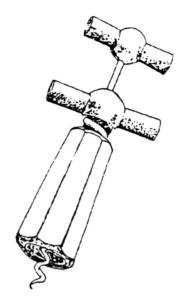

This two-pronged extractor is particularly useful for corks that are likely to crumble. The longer prong is inserted first, then the other. The prongs grip the cork and a slight turn of the handle enables the cork to be extracted. (This type of corkscrew is also known as 'the bad butler's friend'.)

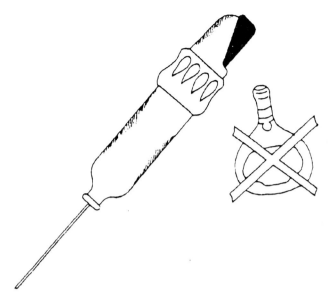

This is a modern type of cork remover for use only on still wines in standard-shaped (cylindrical) full bottles. The needle is inserted into the centre of the cork, the black button pressed once to inject carbon dioxide (CO_2) gas from a Sparklet bulb (type used to make soda water). The pressure of the compressed gas then raises the cork. Another type of remover forces air through the needle by means of a pumping action to raise the cork.

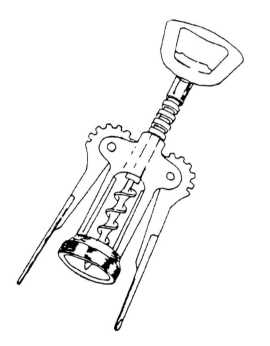

A butterfly cork extractor. The screw is inserted, then the side levers are lowered to pull out. The top of the extractor is a lever for 'crown' corks as found on bottled beer and carbonated juices.

PROCEDURE FOR OPENING WINE

It is important to follow the correct procedure when opening a bottle of wine.

Remove the capsule below the lip of bottle or remove completely if you prefer

Always hold the bottle with a napkin and wipe the top of the cork after the capsule has been removed

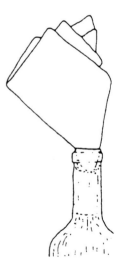

Holding the bottle firmly, gently insert the screw of the corkscrew and gradually extract the cork

Remove the cork from the bottle gently

Wipe the inside of the bottle lip before pouring

DIFFICULT CORKS

If the cork is very tough, insert the corkscrew diagonally, so as to lever the cork out, and push the bottle down at the same time as pulling the screw upwards. Remove the cork. If the cork is broken, inserting the screw diagonally usually extracts the cork.

 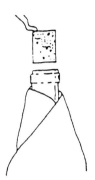

OPENING SPARKLING WINE

Sparkling wine should be cooled by submerging it in ice and water (never ice alone) in a wine cooler or ice bucket. Sparkling wine usually has a cork held in place by a wire muzzle, covered in foil.

When opening sparkling wine, always use a napkin to cover the bottle. This helps provide a good grip and protects your hand if the bottle splits. Study the diagram below to see how to open a bottle of sparkling wine correctly. The napkin has been omitted so that you can see the correct method more clearly.

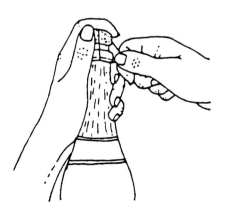

Untwine the wire hook securing the muzzle underneath the capsule. This is usually done anti-clockwise. From this moment, never let go of the cork.

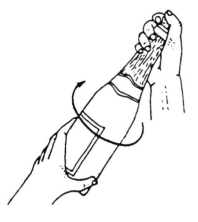

Holding the bottle firmly at a slight angle and not pointing it at anyone or anything breakable, turn the bottle. If you turn the cork, you will risk breaking off the top of the 'mushroom'). When the cork begins to move, continue to hold it until it comes out gently into your hand and doesn't fly up in the air.

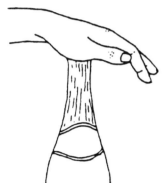

Have a glass ready to take the first rush of bubbles, but if the wine is extra lively and threatens to foam down the side of the bottle, pat the top of the bottle with the palm of your hand. This will prevent any loss of wine.

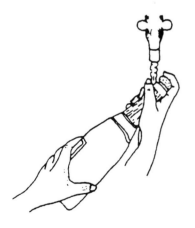

If the cork refuses to budge, run hot water onto the neck of the bottle just below the cork for a few seconds. Hang onto the cork so that it does not fly out.

OPENING FINE WINE

Red wine that has been maturing in the bottle for many years usually contains a deposit known as sediment.

If the wine has been stored correctly on its side, the sediment will have collected to one side of the bottle.

It is important to remove the wine from the bottle without disturbing the sediment.
The wine is usually put in a wine basket to keep the bottle horizontal. If the sediment is heavy, e.g. in the case of vintage port, the wine should be decanted.

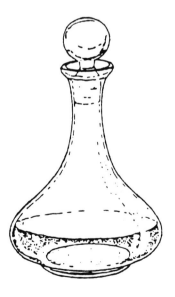

DECANTING

Decanters have several uses. They look attractive on the table. Young red wine can improve if it is decanted, and so exposed to air for a short time before service. The main purpose of decanting wine, however, is to separate the wine from its sediment. Old wine should not be decanted more than an hour before it is to be drunk.

The wine, should be kept in a horizontal position and poured slowly into a decanter or carafe. Sometimes a decanting funnel is used for easier pouring.

A lit candle held under the bottle helps to show when the sediment is nearing the shoulder of the bottle. It is essential to stop pouring at this stage.

Serving wine

ROSÉ OR WHITE WINES

The correct way to serve rosé and white wine:
- Offer the wine list to the customer. Allow the host time to consider the list before ordering. Offer advice if required.
- Stand to the right of the host to take the order.
- Write the order. Give the top copy to the bar and the duplicate to the cashier.
- Place the correct glasses on the table.
- Collect the wine from the dispense bar. Check that it is the correct wine order.
- Take the wine to the table in an ice bucket filled to the shoulder of the bottle with ice and water.
- Present the wine to the host on a clean napkin, showing the label on the bottle so that the host can check his/her choice.
- Place the ice bucket to the right of the host.
- Place a clean white napkin over the handle of the ice bucket.
- Cut the capsule 2 cm below the top of the bottle and remove it.
- Wipe the top of the cork with a napkin.
- Remove the cork from the wine.
- Smell the cork in case the wine is 'corked' (wine is affected by a faulty cork and cannot be served). If it is a chateau-bottled wine, place the cork on a coaster at the top of the host's cover.
- Wipe the top and the inside of the neck of the bottle with a napkin.
- Wipe the bottle dry.
- Hold the bottle so that the host can read the label. Place your right index finger vertically over the shoulder of the bottle.
- Pour a taste for the host (approximately 3 cm) pouring from the right-hand side. The host should acknowledge that the wine is suitable, having the correct taste,

bouquet and temperature.
- As you finish pouring, gently twist the neck of the bottle to the right as you raise it to prevent drips falling onto the tablecloth.
- Pour the wine for the lady on the right of the host, filling the glass two-thirds full.
- Proceed to the right, working round the table, serving the ladies first. Continue round the table, serving the gentlemen, leaving the host until last. Fill his/her glass to the same level.
- Replace the bottle in the ice bucket and refill glass when necessary.
- If fresh bottle is required, place fresh glasses on the table.

RED WINES

Red wine should be served in a similar way. The main differences are that:
- It should be served from a decanter or opened and served from a wine cradle.
- It should be served at 'room temperature'. This can vary from approximately 12°C for light young red wines to 18°C for full-bodied red wines. (See table on page 142).

ELEMENT 2C6.1 *Prepare and serve bottled wines*

1   Part of the enjoyment of having a glass of wine is the temperature that wine should be served at. What are the ideal service temperatures of the following wines?

A young white wine ....

A sweet white wine ....

A young red wine ....

A 'heavy' red wine..

A sparkling wine...

A dry fortified wine ....

A sweet fortified wine ....

2 From your own wine list draw up a guide with the following information:

Wine	Region	Sales Description	Alternative

3 Draw up a chart, either a bar graph or a pie chart, which illustrates the popularity of each of the wines on your list. The numbers can then be converted into percentages of the total wines sold.

4 From the above chart what are the most popular: white, red, rosé or sparkling wines? Can you ascertain why one wine would appear to be more popular than others? Is the popularity based on price or value for money, special offers, use of 'tent cards/promotions', themed events in your restaurant?

   ....

   ....

5 Draw up a checklist that shows the step-by-step approach to the preparation and service of the following wines to customers:

   White wine

   ....

   ....

Red wine

....

....

....

Rosé wine

....

....

....

Sparkling wine

....

....

....

6   Before a wine waiter commences service he/she must ensure that everything required for service is to hand. List the points that you think are important to smooth service.

....

....

....

....

....

....

....

7   Read the following sentences carefully and insert the missing words in the blanks provided.

THE SERVICE OF WINE

The wine list should always be presented to the .... of a group of people. He/she should be allowed time to .... the list before ordering, and receive .... offered by the wine waiter on the choice of wine, if requested. The wine glasses used should always be large enough to hold sufficient wine when .... full. Glasses should be highly .... with a clean .... before use. The bottle should be .... to the host before preparing for its service to ensure that it is of the correct type ordered.

Unless otherwise directed, white wine should be............................ by placing it in .... Red wine should normally be served at .... temperature.

When preparing to remove the cork, the corkscrew should not pass through the bottom of the cork or pieces of .... will fall into the wine. The screw should pass through the .... of the cork. When removed, the cork should be .... to check for .... Before serving, the .... should be given opportunity to .... the wine to check that it is acceptable to him/her. When wine is decanted, care must be taken not to disturb the ....

Record of Achievement – Completion of Unit 2C6

Candidate's signature   ....

Assessor's signature   ....

Date   ....
